Online Benefits Technology

The Strategic Broker's Guide

Alex Tolbert

authorHOUSE®

AuthorHouse™
1663 Liberty Drive
Bloomington, IN 47403
www.authorhouse.com
Phone: 1 (800) 839-8640

Published by AuthorHouse   12/08/2017

ISBN: 978-1-5246-5550-1 (sc)
ISBN: 978-1-5246-5549-5 (e)

Library of Congress Control Number: 2016920980

Print information available on the last page.

Any people depicted in stock imagery provided by Thinkstock are models,
and such images are being used for illustrative purposes only.
Certain stock imagery © Thinkstock.

This book is printed on acid-free paper.

Contents

For health insurance brokers and advisors everywhere –
whose work is so important and so personal.

Introduction

2006 was the year I got my start in health insurance. The prior year I had run the cafe at my school, an experience that turned me onto the idea of being an entrepreneur. Still a student with one year left in my program, my health law classes had me pretty stirred up about all of the misaligned incentives in healthcare. Health Savings Accounts (HSAs) were relatively new at the time, and a concept that I thought was the first step to realigning those incentives.

My first idea was to start a bank that focused on Health Savings Accounts. A price comparison tool for healthcare was another idea. Nashville-based venture capitalist Bill Cook asked me what kind of business I would start around HSAs if I wasn't going to raise any money at all — that question spurred me to decide to get my health insurance license and be a broker.

As a broker, I'd be on the front lines and would figure out why employers were not adopting HSAs as quickly as many policy analysts had expected. I'd explain to them what it meant for the healthcare system. I'd help spur the change so many believe needs to happen to make our healthcare system more effective.

And so with those inspirational thoughts in mind, I got my insurance license, put together my presentation on the history of healthcare and how HSAs were the key to making things better, and started calling employers to spread the word and become their broker.

I started to sense my own naivety when I wasn't getting any clients. The employers I met with were all respectful. They listened to my "pitch" and would even share their own healthcare frustrations with me. But they didn't hire me.

Until Becky Sharpe. The visionary owner of Scholarship Program Administrators, which has since changed its name to International Scholarship and Tuition Services, hired me on the spot. She had read about HSAs herself and recently had tried to implement them. Only two out of her 14 employees took the HSA option and her broker had told her that any money not spent from the HSA would automatically go into employees' 401(k). Remember, this was 2006 when HSAs were still new for everyone.

In order for HSAs to really work for Becky's company, I recommended that she change to a different insurance company that offered more favorable HSA-based plan designs. She agreed. The amount of paperwork that ensued was amazing. What was more amazing to me was that all parties — Becky, her office manager, the insurance company — seemed to be on the same page that the paperwork was my responsibility. Remember, I had become a broker for the noble pursuit of improving the U.S. healthcare system, not to process paperwork. But given this was my first client, I was all over it. I checked to make sure every "i" was dotted and "t" crossed — and still missed things.

Eventually, though, the paperwork got squared away, the rates finalized, and I got the opportunity to present the new, HSA-based plan to Becky's employees. They loved it. Becky was saving so much in premiums that she was able to help fund the employees' HSAs so that everyone could win. They all agreed that I explained it much better than the prior broker. It felt good.

A few days later, Becky's office manager called me. She was frustrated. Employees had made their elections, but she wasn't sure when to start making the deductions from their paychecks. And how was the employer's HSA contribution supposed to be reflected in their payroll system? And could employees just change their HSA deduction whenever they wanted? Why was her payroll company telling her she needed more than one payroll deduction code to accommodate HSAs? Also, how were the contributions supposed to be made to the bank? Finally, the accountant wanted records for where all of this money was going — how were these reports supposed to be made efficiently?

As I was listening to her, I remember wondering why these questions were being directed to me. Wasn't I supposed to be the healthcare advisor? What did that have to do with payroll deduction codes? But I drove out to meet with the office manager, and helped her through all of these questions. At the time I figured it was just one needy client, and the time spent well worth it as I was trying to get my business going.

But then it was the same thing with my second client. And my third. And fourth. Every client had these issues, and they all expected me to resolve them.

I eventually began to appreciate that the small employers I was calling on did not see it as their responsibility to fix the U.S. healthcare system. They had their own problems to deal with. I wanted to be their trusted healthcare advisor, but if I didn't meet them where they were, they were not going to let me have that role. Around this time my brother, Brian, joined me in the effort and we agreed that it was our job to solve as many problems as we could for our clients.

Because so many of a small employer's most acute, day-to-day healthcare headaches are transactional in nature, we learned that meeting our prospects where they were meant addressing transactional as well as strategic problems. That insight is what eventually caused building

BerniePortal, the web-based HR and Benefits platform built in harmony for brokers, employers, and employees.

As someone who has thought about and worked on this problem for the last ten years, in the rest of this book I'm going to share:

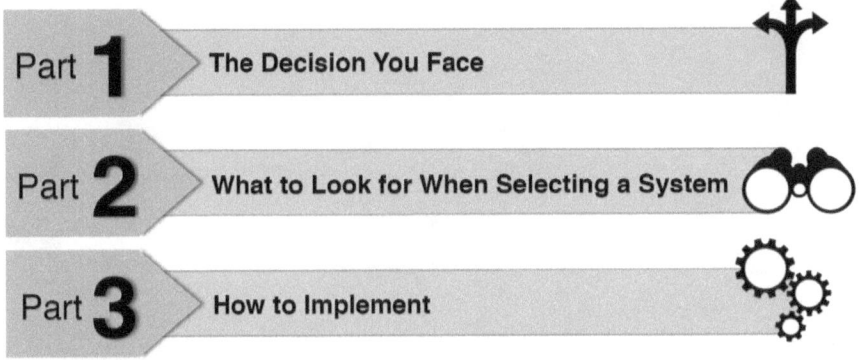

Part **1**   The Decision You Face

Part **2**   What to Look for When Selecting a System

Part **3**   How to Implement

I'll also share some anecdotes along the way — both from my time working as a broker and from my experience as part of the team building BerniePortal. Whether BerniePortal ends up being the right system for you and your agency or not, I think you'll find that the insights we've worked hard to develop over the last ten years and are sharing here will be helpful to you in your agency's journey.

Part 1:

The Decision You Face

1 | Let Them Pick or Select One for Them?

Bottom line: The decision you and all agencies who serve the 10 to 500 segment face is whether to select an online benefits system for your clients, or let them all go pick their own.

Either way you go has dramatic implications. The urgency to make a decision is at its height, as we're on the cusp of a huge move by these small employers to administer their benefits online.

Skeptical? Feel like you've heard that the move online is imminent for ten years and nothing has happened? Fact: Disruptive innovations are always things that people in the industry talk about for years before they actually happen. Then, when they do, they happen in a flash.

Online benefits technology is at the cusp of that flash. How do we know? We know because the market is close to fulfilling the entire promise of the technology. Once the entire promise is fulfilled, everyone moves. Innovation thought leaders like Geoffrey Moore have compared the moment when the technology finally fulfills the entire promise to being like a tornado.

What is the promise of benefits technology? Here is a sampling:

1. Process open enrollment
2. Process qualifying events
3. Integrate with the insurance companies
4. Be or integrate with payroll
5. Provide multimedia education about benefits offerings
6. Allow a multitude of benefit funding strategies
7. Help agencies more effectively manage their businesses
8. Produce insurance company bills
9. Be and integrate with COBRA provider
10. 1094-C / 1095-C
11. Be compatible with the entire HR ecosystem

1 Process open enrollment

2 Process qualifying events

3 Integrate with the insurance companies

4 Be or integrate with payroll

5 Provide multimedia education about benefits offerings

6 Allow a multitude of benefit funding strategies

7 Help agencies more effectively manage their businesses

8 Produce insurance company bills

9 Be and integrate with COBRA provider

10 1094-C / 1095-C

11 Be compatible with the entire HR ecosystem

Most of this list has been talked about for years, but for a variety of reasons the market was not able to produce a solution that did it all. Today, however, we are on the cusp of the market finally producing products that fulfill the promise. Let's review each of these 11 items one by one.

Open enrollment and qualifying events. Being able to process open enrollment and qualifying events is now not such a big deal, but five years ago there were plenty of platforms on the market — that had customers — that could only do open enrollment.

Integrating with insurance companies. This is still a challenge, but the market is getting close on this. Many platforms can offer it for any group over 100 lives with any carrier, and then select carries down to five lives. Expect the number of "select carriers" to broaden so that soon all platforms will be able to offer it with all carriers. Otherwise, some platforms are now printing employee elections on the insurance company forms so that those can be submitted automatically if an actual integration is not possible.

Payroll integration. Historically, payroll companies were not able to integrate with benefits technology platforms. ADP is leading change in this area with the ADP Marketplace. As of this writing, there are two benefit technology platforms on the ADP Marketplace that can offer full integration with ADP's Workforce Now payroll product. Other payroll companies are rolling out similar efforts to integrate.

Multimedia education about benefit offerings. People want more than just a PDF — they want to be able to write notes about the benefit offerings and even provide videos and in some cases avatars. Most of the systems on the market today now address this.

Allow a multitude of benefit funding strategies. Brokers are creative problem-solvers. As a result, employers fund their benefits programs in a dizzying myriad of ways. Want to fund your plan based on a fixed percentage that you pay towards the "employee only" tier of a certain base plan? Want that fixed percentage to be different for employees versus spouses versus children? Want just a defined contribution from the employer available for the employee to spend on any benefit? Want that just for non-medical benefits? Want multiple defined contributions available for different buckets of benefits? For a system to truly work for health insurance agencies, they need their system to be able to do it all because their employer clients are doing it all. Today's leading platforms now address all of this.

Help agencies more effectively manage their business. The promise of benefits technology is that it will help the employer as well as its broker. Because all of an agency's clients can be on one platform, it makes sense that the platform should have tools built-in to help the agency better manage its book of business. This means making it easier to provide top-notch customer service, to report to clients on what service requests were handled, to track commissions the agency is owed by its carriers, to run quotes at renewal, and to help employer clients expand their benefits offering to include more types of benefits. The top platforms being considered by agencies today are increasingly checking these items off the list.

Produce insurance company bills. Consolidated billing has been desired by employers and their brokers since the 1970s. This is in part because of how painful it is to audit insurance company bills that are so often wrong. With online benefits technology, getting a correct bill every time can be a cinch if the online benefits system itself simply produces the bill. After all, it is already the system of record for eligibility whenever it is integrated with a carrier. Leading carriers are recognizing this and turning over billing responsibilities to the benefits technology firms. Unum, the leading disability carrier for over 40 years, has shown great leadership in this area. Others are following quickly.

Be or integrate with the COBRA provider. COBRA is one of those things that can cause huge administrative headaches and just be an enormous drain on time. You think you're through open enrollment for a complicated,

300 life group and then someone asks "Wait, did we communicate with our seven COBRA enrollees about the new carrier and plan offerings?" Benefits technology allows the COBRA enrollees to make their elections in the same system as the active workers, getting the same notifications about when elections can be made. Again— today's leading platforms now have this built-in.

1094-C/1095-C. The government requirement to report on employee health coverage caused a slew of software vendors to rise up as standalone 1094-C/1095-C providers. Long-term, these make about as much sense as a standalone W-2 provider. Payroll providers naturally generate the W-2 at the end of the year because they've been tracking pay all year. Similarly, the benefits platform will ultimately, and naturally, generate the 1095-Cs every year as it has been tracking benefits and coverage. Almost all of the top benefits platforms understood this and addressed it with their product.

Be compatible with the entire HR ecosystem. Applicant tracking, onboarding, benefits, payroll, time and attendance, paid time off, performance tracking, offboarding — each one of these items is a separate set of processes that HR has to manage. Benefits affects nearly all of them in one way or another. Think variable hour tracking, and you'll get a sense of how benefits touches everything. The full promise of online benefits technology includes it working well with these other parts of the HR ecosystem. To varying degrees and with different approaches, this is happening.

In addition to the fact that the entire promise of online benefits technology is so close to being fulfilled, there is another important factor at play.

Millennials.

You know them. For many of you reading, they are your children or grandchildren. Digital natives, they are often astonished (in a bad way) at how benefits are administered today. Paper processes, spreadsheets. Their reaction is visceral — for some, it is enough to make them want to throw up.

And they're getting older. With age comes power, and as they move into roles at their organizations with more decision-making power they are increasingly insisting that the paper be tossed in favor of moving online.

Investors have seen all of this, and are responding by writing checks. Lots of checks for lots of money. Over $1 billion of venture capital financing has poured into companies that provide some semblance of online benefits technology to the 10-500 employee employer segment. These companies have big marketing budgets and are great at advertising online — whatever it takes to find themselves in front of your clients.

And this is in addition to the efforts of existing players — namely payroll companies — who are working furiously to build online benefits systems that they can sell alongside of payroll.

Which leads us to the biggest decision health insurance agencies that serve the 10 to 500 employee segment face over the next five years.

Do you let your clients pick their own benefit systems or do you select a system and incorporate it as part of the value proposition you deliver to your clients?

In other words, let clients pick or select a system for them?

Estimates vary, but the range most agree on is that there are between 20,000 and 30,000 health insurance agencies in the United States. Some percentage of agencies will select a system and provide it as part of their value proposition. Others will let, or even encourage, their clients to pick their own systems.

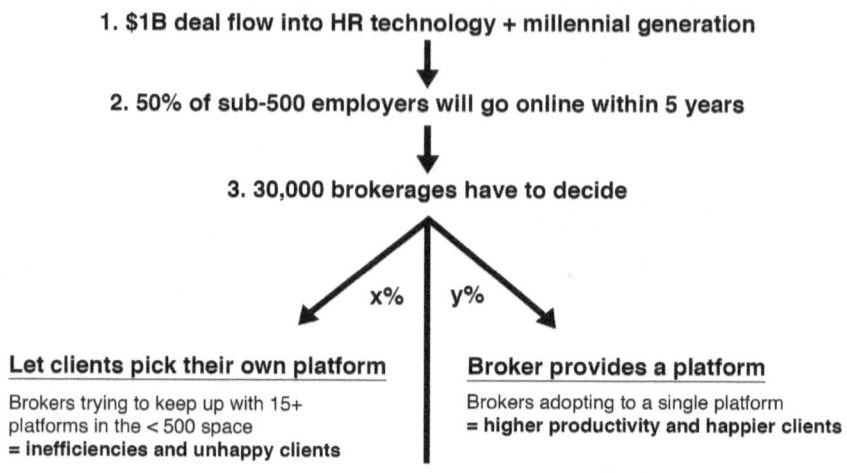

1. $1B deal flow into HR technology + millennial generation

2. 50% of sub-500 employers will go online within 5 years

3. 30,000 brokerages have to decide

x%   y%

Let clients pick their own platform

Brokers trying to keep up with 15+
platforms in the < 500 space
= inefficiencies and unhappy clients

Broker provides a platform

Brokers adopting to a single platform
= higher productivity and happier clients

The agencies who select a system and implement it successfully will experience huge success. Happier clients, more clients, and a doubling of profitability (more on all of that later). The agencies who let their clients all pick a system will flounder and ultimately die.

The difference really is that stark. Why?

There are two important facts to keep in mind when thinking about this:

1. Employers want a competitive benefit package at an affordable cost that can be administered with minimal hassle
2. Employers won't build out their own benefit systems

Let's take the first fact first. Employers in the 10 to 500 segment really don't care about all of the myriad features of "Benefit System A" versus "Benefit System B" versus "Benefit System C." If you ask them they might say they do, but they don't. Or at least not versus their highest want, which is to have a competitive benefit package at an affordable cost with minimal hassle. You already know this, but I'm emphasizing it because we understand the tendency to think it would be best to let clients pick their own systems based on the mistaken premise that they all may prefer different things. They don't. They all want the same thing. Competitive package, affordable cost, minimal hassle. You're their broker, they expect you to deliver that for them.

That takes us to the second fact: Employers will not build out their own benefit systems. Every year at open enrollment the plans and deduction amounts change. New benefits are added, maybe some are no longer offered. Someone has to update the benefits system to account for the changes. The employer won't do it. Invariably, the responsibility falls to the agency.

In other words, your agency will ultimately be supporting your client's benefit system whether you provided it or they picked it on their own. If you refuse to support a system they picked on their own, they'll find a broker who will.

With this in mind, let's look at each scenario.

Scenario 1: Let clients pick

How many systems can your team reliably support for your small employer clients?

The answer to that question is one. Just one.

Do you have an iPhone? Did you ever use Android? Have you gone back and forth?

Or are you a Mac user? Have you recently tried to use a PC or vice versa?

With technology, even though systems may ultimately be designed to achieve similar outcomes, the approaches they take are often entirely different. As a result, it is difficult for even the most tech-savvy professional to manage multiple different systems reliably.

Imagine that you let your clients pick and they end up on ten different platforms. How is your team supposed to keep up with all of the updates and improvements those ten different systems make on an ongoing basis?

And then what happens when they can't, and so they end up not managing a client's system reliably? Mistakes. Incorrect deductions, mismanaged open enrollments. Bottom line: frustration for everyone and lost clients.

Remember this: The same client you bent over backwards for to help them pick their own system will be furious with you — and blame you — if their open enrollment doesn't go smoothly.

Okay, so now let's look at the other option.

Scenario 2: Select a system for your clients

This is where you select a system and implement it successfully by incorporating it into your value proposition.

In this scenario, your team takes time to understand the system you've selected. You identify how you can improve your agency's own internal processes as it relates to processing renewals, implementing new clients, preparing for employee open enrollment communications, handling adds, terms, and changes, and who is responsible for what. With confidence, you implement with clients in the manner that maximizes the likelihood of successful adoption (more on that later — how to implement with clients successfully is counterintuitive for most agencies).

In this scenario, open enrollments run smoothly because your team knows what it is doing and has confidence in its system. Clients are happy and so more likely to stay with you and refer you to friends. They also begin offering more lines of coverage, as participation requirements and concerns about administrative costs related to more benefits melt away and they see the value of offering a package as robust as the large employer with whom they compete for talent. Your close ratio with prospects goes up, as you begin to position your agency as addressing both their acute, transactional challenges with software and their long-term, strategic challenges with your strategic mind, experience, and problem-solving ability coupled with the best service and a strong relationship.

Sounds pretty good, right? So what is the downside?

Downsides of selecting a platform for your clients

The first downside is that this is going to be a lot of work. In fact, in the early months it will feel like you're not making progress and things are actually worse. Many refer to this period of technology adoption as the "valley of despair."

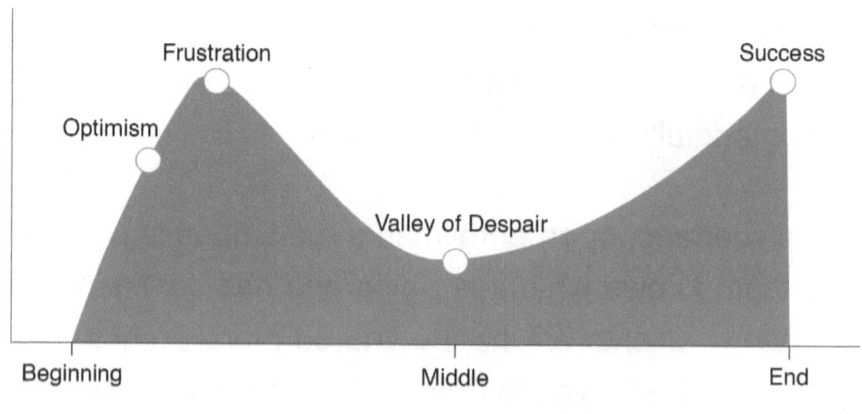

Valley of Despair

The valley of despair is not fun. The other side of the valley, though, is well worth it. Indeed, it will prove to be transformational for your agency once you've helped your clients move online. But it will take work.

The other downside of selecting a platform is that awful, anxious feeling that you might select the wrong one. You select the wrong platform, work hard to implement it with your clients, and watch as it doesn't make the investments necessary in product or support to stay as cutting-edge as it seemed when you originally selected it. Other systems — systems you passed on when you selected yours — ultimately outshine your system leaving you at a disadvantage versus other agencies who happened to select the "right" system.

This is a risk. There is no doubt about it. In some ways it seems like it would be easier to wait to select a system for your agency until a market leader or leaders have emerged. A system that is more clearly going to be around for the long haul and make those important investments in its product and support teams to stay as cutting edge as the day you signed up.

Certainly the majority of agencies are in this boat right now.

The thing that makes waiting so tricky is that those millennials are not getting any younger. Those venture capitalists aren't known to be especially patient for their investments to pay off. In other words — whether you select a system or not, your clients are going to begin getting online with or without you. As that happens, you risk inadvertently putting your agency in that dreaded position of being expected to maintain multiple benefits systems for clients who all picked their own.

How risky it is to wait depends on how many clients you have who are inclined to move online. This can be difficult to judge. Even your most blue collar client may surprise you with a move online without you if the owner's 27-year-old daughter moves back home and takes over HR.

We're going to cover what to look for in selecting a system more extensively in Part 2. Rest assured, though, that this market is big enough that there will be multiple "winners" among the benefits technology firms. Furthermore, we are finding at BerniePortal that the same four or five systems seem to be the ones being evaluated every time we talk to a broker. In other words, the risk of choosing wrong is a lot lower today than it was even just a few years ago.

Before we get into what to look for when picking a system, let's dive a bit deeper into the day-to-day life of our employer clients and the HR ecosystem they navigate. We're going to do this for a few reasons. First, it will deepen your understanding of the transactional pain your clients are going through related to HR and give you more confidence that change is in the air in the next five years. Second, when your clients move benefits online — with or without you — it impacts their entire HR ecosystem. You'll be a more valuable extension of your client's team the more you understand how.

2 | Why the HR Ecosystem is the Way it is Today

The HR ecosystem today is largely made up of paper-based processes and spreadsheets. The work is often very tedious. This is true everywhere in the ecosystem except for payroll, which is often outsourced to a third party.

Let's review the ecosystem through the lens of Acme Company, employer of 45 employees, recruiting for a new customer service position at Acme. James Toms is the office manager who maintains Acme's HR ecosystem.

First, the hiring manager for the new position gets with James to write a job description. The owner of the company wants to see the job description as well. In the job description they write that the company offers a robust benefits package, including health insurance. Proud of what they've written, they agree that James should post it on the various job websites and then coordinate with the hiring manager on progress. The owner says she also wants to be kept in the loop.

James dutifully posts the job on Indeed, LinkedIn, Monster, and CareerBuilder. And it turns out they did a great job writing the job description — the applications come roaring in! James does a preliminary screen of the resumes, and then forwards the good ones to the hiring manager, copying the owner. Internal correspondence ensues as they communicate about which resumes are good enough to qualify for the next step in the hiring process.

James emails back the people whose resume did not make the cut, and puts those resumes in a "decline" folder within the "Customer Service Position" folder on his desktop.

He then emails each of the eight individuals who did make it to the next step, and he asks those eight individuals to fill out a personality profile as well as write answers to some "written response" prompts an HR consultant had recommended they use.

Six of the eight people respond within a few days with their profile and responses. James creates a folder for each of them within his "Customer Service Position" folder to store this information along with their resumes. He also sends emails to the hiring manger, copying the owner, with "Candidate Name: Profile and Responses" in the subject line. Correspondence ensues about who they should bring in for an interview.

James then sets up interviews with the four candidates that they had agreed over email should be brought in. One declines, leaving three who agree to come in to be interviewed. In one of the interviews a promising candidate asks about the healthcare benefits. James leaves the room to go gather some materials leftover from the open enrollment meetings to try to describe the benefits. The candidate had some further questions that required James to call their broker to get answers.

Ultimately, the company decides to hire Nancy Smith. James is in charge of bringing her on board as a new hire. He has a folder on his desktop called "New hire paperwork." In this folder, he maintains the following:

New Hire Paperwork

☑ A copy of this year's version of the W-4

☑ A copy of this year's version of the I-9

☑ A copy of this year's version of the W-9

☑ A copy of this year's version of his state's witholding paperwork

☑ A copy of his company's direct deposit form

☑ A copy of his company's confidentiality agreement

☑ A copy of his company's employement agreement

☑ A copy of his company's emergency contact form

☑ A copy of his company's employee handbook acknowledgement form

He opens each of the documents that are custom to his company and finds in the document the places that need to be customized for Nancy. He does the customizations, and then saves each document in a new folder that he has created called "Nancy Smith New Hire Paperwork."

Next, he emails Nancy. In the email he explains that she needs to fill out the 9 pieces of attached paperwork and either email them back or bring with her on her first day.

Nancy is very conscientious, and so she prints out all of the paperwork, fills it out, and then scans and emails it back to James the day before her first day.

James and Nancy meet the first day to review the paperwork. Unfortunately, most of it is not filled out correctly. James reprints the paperwork and they spend about an hour filling it out together.

In this meeting, Nancy asks about the healthcare benefits. She was not the one who asked about them during the interview process. James tries to explain all of the options, and again tries to cobble together some materials leftover from the last open enrollment meetings. Nancy has a few questions that require James to call the broker to get answers. All of this takes another hour.

Acme Company has a waiting period of FOM 60 days, so James and Nancy agree that it's not necessary for her to sign up for anything right then. Besides, they are both exhausted from filling things out. They agree they'll get the benefit sign-ups done closer to the date that she is eligible for them, which is May 1st.

James then also explains how she is supposed to fill out an Excel spreadsheet to report her hours worked, and the circumstances under which she is allowed to work overtime. He explains that Nancy is to email him each week with her timesheet, which he then compiles for processing payroll. James also explains how to request paid time off and how that is tracked in the spreadsheet he has designed for that purpose. If it is possible that Nancy will work fewer than 30 hours on a regular basis, James explains how that would impact her eligibility for benefits.

Nancy leaves to meet with her new boss. James turns to the paperwork and begins the process of getting Nancy set up in Acme's payroll system.

Acme Company uses ADP for payroll. Because it has employees in multiple states, they use ADP's Workforce Now product. James walks through the "new hire" wizard to load in all of Nancy's pertinent information.

About 45 days go by and it is April 10th. Nancy comes by James's desk and asks about signing up for benefits. James agrees it is about time that they get that done. He explains to Nancy that he just needs her to make choices and turn in the paperwork to him. Nancy apologizes, but she misplaced the paperwork that James gave her on her first day. James has run out of copies of some of it, and so he emails his broker to ask for electronic copies that he can print out.

A few days later, James has given Nancy all of the information and enrollment forms for each carrier. Nancy takes it home to review with her husband and make choices. They decide they should compare the options to what they get through Nancy's husband's employer. Getting that information together takes a few days. They figure it is not a big deal because, after all, they don't have to decide until May 1st. They eventually get the information and end up deciding that Nancy should go on Acme's plan and her husband will stay on his employer's plan.

Nancy takes the paperwork in to James on April 23rd. James reviews it and, it looking good to him, he scans and emails it to his broker's office. His broker catches some errors, which James works with Nancy to correct. Eventually, the information gets to the carriers and James enters it in payroll.

Other than Nancy not filling out the new hire paperwork correctly, the above illustrates the best case scenario for what happens at most of America's small employers when it comes to getting a new hire up and running. It doesn't even cover the back-and-forth that occurs related to benefits open enrollment or qualifying events and tracking hours worked or PTO. But you get the idea. Your clients' HR ecosystem is mired in manual processes. They need help from someone to get those processes to be more automated online.

They're going to get that help from someone, and for the reasons we'll discuss in the next chapter, their health insurance broker is the one in the best position to supply it.

Before we get into that, though, it's important to understand not just how the HR ecosystem works, but why the HR ecosystem is the way that it is. The HR ecosystem is the way that it is today for three reasons:

1. World War II
2. High degree of complexity
3. "Cost center" mentality

Let's start with how World War II contributed to shaping the way the HR ecosystem is today.

Reason 1: World War II

World War II was very expensive for the United States. As a result, there was a lot of pressure on the government to collect more tax revenue.

Before the war, the federal income tax only affected a small percentage of citizens — most of whom were very wealthy. These individuals generally paid their taxes in one lump sum, once per year. It is estimated that only about 4 percent of the population had to pay this tax.

In order to finance the cost of the war, the government expanded who it taxed so that a far greater percentage of the population had to pay income taxes. Millions of people who had never had to pay income taxes before now had to be able to pay a hefty annual income tax bill. These new taxpayers were overwhelmed by both the complexity of the returns and the size of the annual bill. Many did not have the money to pay their income tax bill when it became due.

Collecting from individuals was such a problem that the government decided to change course, and force employers to withhold the amount of income taxes an individual owed on a given paycheck from the individual. Then, the employer would turn that money over to the government on the individual's behalf. The government did this with the Current Tax Payment Act of 1943.

In other words, the government shifted the burden of compliance and payment from the individual to the employer.

And it was a heavy burden. Employers hated it. Even at a time of heightened patriotism due to the war effort, employers resented this new requirement. To make it even worse, there were stiff penalties if an employer screwed it up or didn't comply.

Out of this government action to fund World War II grew today's payroll industry. By the end of the 1940s, ADP had been founded so that employers could outsource the burden of withholding to a third party. Roughly ten years after that, ADP went public. Another ten or so years later, an ADP employee left to found a company focused on smaller employers. That's Paychex.

The HR ecosystem involves an array of systems. Applicant tracking. New hire onboarding. Benefits administration. Payroll. Paid time off. Time and attendance. Offboarding.

Of all of these systems, payroll is the one that is most often outsourced. Government action caused that to happen, and government rules and regulations cause it to be very important that the information in the payroll system be correct. The impact on the HR ecosystem is still felt today.

Reason 2: High degree of complexity

HR is simply a lot more complex than other parts of a business. Because it is more complex, it is more difficult to build software that addresses HR's needs. As a result, most parts of the HR ecosystem are still managed with paper and spreadsheets.

Don't believe that HR is more complex than other parts of a business? Let's look at sales for the sake of comparison. It is also instructive to look at sales because most businesses today run their sales processes on a software platform.

First, the VP of Sales for a company only needs her software to contemplate the needs of her salespeople. This is just a small proportion of the overall employee base. HR has to worry about everyone.

The VP of Sales also doesn't need her software to accommodate people who aren't with the company yet or people who have left. HR does.

Now, let's talk about what the VP of Sales does need. She needs her software to maintain a database of leads. She needs to be able to indicate what the various stages are before a lead really engages in a buying process. Once the lead has engaged in the buying process, the VP of Sales needs to be able to see a pipeline report with projected close dates. She then needs reports tracking various metrics during the buying cycle. Every dependency in the system is completely controlled by the VP of Sales. In other words, the VP of Sales decides what action causes a lead to be considered to have "engaged" in the buying process. The VP of Sales decides what is considered to be a "closed won" deal. Sales does not really need its system to integrate with any other system. Integrating with marketing would be nice, but not necessary to get a lot of value.

Let's contrast this with what HR needs — ignoring completely the payroll system. The HR/Benefits system first needs to communicate various government forms (W-4, I-9, state withholding) to new hires and get them completed. It needs to collect signatures on many of these forms from the new hire as well as others at the company or elsewhere. It needs to communicate other new hire forms that are custom to the company and perhaps different for different sets of employees. It needs to get the new hire's information into payroll. And to benefits. And paid time off. And time and attendance. It needs to communicate to the employees what the benefits options are and collect benefit elections from those employees. It needs to get the payroll deductions into payroll and communicate the benefit elections to the various insurance companies. It needs to track how many hours employees are working, and get into payroll the number of hours each week and whether any of them were overtime hours. It needs to make sure people are taking a lunch break if they are supposed to take a lunch break. It needs to track how much paid time off an employee has accrued.

And we're only barely getting started. The system also needs to allow employees to request time off and approvers to be able to approve after making sure not too many people are going to be out on the same day. It needs to maintain a personnel file on the employee, including keeping I-9s separate and enabling the employee to see sections of their file — but not all of it. It needs to help in tracking performance and compensation changes. It needs to communicate benefits open enrollment changes every year and collect deductions and transmit changes to carriers. It needs to generate 1094-Cs and 1095-Cs for distribution to employees and submission to the government. And finally it needs to communicate with the COBRA vendor when the employee leaves. As far dependencies, the HR and benefits system is riddled with complicated dependencies, many of which HR doesn't have the power to just "choose." Government and insurance company rules dictate a lot, and they are a mishmash that can vary from one state to the next and one carrier to the next. And when it comes to integrations — HR needs them in droves. It needs this system to integrate with payroll as well as with all of the insurance companies and other systems.

Bottom line: What HR needs is a lot more complicated than what Sales needs when it comes to software. For this reason, it has proven more difficult for software companies to build a "whole solution" that meets all of an employer's needs. That is the second reason the HR ecosystem is the way that it is today.

Reason 3: "Cost center" mentality

HR professionals are fully aware that it is difficult to draw a straight line in between the important work they do and revenue growth at an organization. As a result, many organizations classify HR as a "cost center" — a place to work on managing costs rather than making investments.

That doesn't bode well for investments in online HR software in general. And it is even worse for investment in online benefits technology. Because the insurance companies and agencies also gain efficiencies from online benefits technology, employers often feel like they should be paying for it. Developers of sales software live in a world where Salesforce.com is able to charge over $100 per employee per month for a license. Developers of HR software live in a world where employers balk at paying even 10 percent of that.

This is the third reason for an HR ecosystem riddled with paper processes outside of payroll. Not only is the software that HR needs extremely difficult to build, but organizations are simply not willing to pay a lot for it.

3 | The Healthcare Advisor's Role in Solving for HR's Transactional Challenges

We've covered the degree to which the HR ecosystem is mired in manual processes and why that is the case. America's small businesses are going to get help from someone to automate their processes online. The party in the best position to help them do that is the health insurance broker.

Why?

Because of the following truths:

1. Benefits, uniquely, touches almost every single part of the ecosystem
2. The broker has to support the benefits system

3. There is more money in benefits than in any other corner of the ecosystem

We'll review one by one.

<u>Benefits touches almost every single part of the ecosystem</u>

Do job applicants ever want to know what the benefits are at an employer? Yes, sometimes. So benefits touch the applicant tracking system.

Do new hires want to know what the benefits are? Yes, always. So benefits touch onboarding.

Does time and attendance and PTO impact benefits eligibility? Yes, sometimes. So benefits touches those parts of the HR ecosystem.

Does payroll need to know what the pay deductions are for benefits for a given employee? Yes, always. So benefits touches payroll.

When offboarding an employee, is it important to know what benefits they had? Yes, for COBRA purposes as well as notifying the carriers of the term. So benefits touches offboarding.

Benefits is the only aspect of the HR ecosystem that reliably impacts every single other aspect of the ecosystem. As a result, the ideal situation for HR is to be able to rely on whoever supports its benefits system to help it get everything online.

The broker has to support the benefits system

We won't spend much time here, as we've already covered this extensively. HR will not build it out its own benefits system every year. This will always fall to the broker. The broker has to support the benefits system.

Given that the broker has to support the benefits system and HR's ideal environment is one where it can rely on the supporter of its benefits system to help with everything else, one would think the analysis could stop there. But there is one additional and extremely important truth.

There is more money in benefits than in any other corner of the ecosystem

Brokers make a lot of money. Not too much money, just a lot of money. They work extremely hard for it and they can also be fired relatively easily. As a result, HR generally gets what it wants from its broker.

So, if HR wants its broker to support its benefits system and it wants the supporter of its benefits system to assist it with other things – well, that is probably going to happen.

The broker may wonder how she got herself in a position where she is having conversations about how the time and attendance system will assist in variable hour tracking for benefits eligibility. What happened to the days when you just brought the quotes, helped HR choose, and then explained the benefits package to employees?

Those days are over, but it is not all bad. As a broker, you're going to gain a lot from benefits and HR going online, too. After all, your agency's operations are mired in manual processes resulting from the same dynamics that cause your clients' HR ecosystem to be mired in manual processes. As you help your clients go online, you'll go online as well. You going online will allow you to reap an array of benefits, including doubling your profits. Yes, you will be able to double your agency's profits. We'll cover how that will happen in Part III. Before we get to that, though, we'll review in Part II how to evaluate the different systems that are out there and select the right one for you.

Part 2:

What to Look For When Selecting a System

4 | Two Approaches to Building a Benefits System

I know the two approaches to building a benefits system well, as I've been a part of building both. The first approach is called the "benefit-centric" approach. The second is the "employee-centric" approach. In 2008, we built BerniePortal using the "benefit-centric" approach. Then, in 2012 we realized that was a huge mistake and we rebuilt the system using an "employee-centric" approach. That rebuild was extremely painful, and we were only able to do it because, frankly, we didn't have very many users back then and they were all employers for which the agency that my brother, Brian, leads was the broker.

It will become clear why we made the change as I explain how the two approaches work. The bottom line for you is that you want an employee-centric system. A benefit-centric system has some initial appeal. I'll be the first to admit that – after all, it is how we built BerniePortal the first time. But it will cause you all sorts of problems long-term.

Okay, so let's talk about how things look with the benefit-centric approach. Under this approach, you have the following:

1. Timeframes (eligibility rules) are assigned to benefit subgroups
2. Billing codes assigned to benefit subgroups
3. Plans and rates assigned to benefit subgroups
4. Employees are assigned to benefit subgroups

This is a beautiful approach for simple groups. For example, take a group that has:

1. One set of "timeframe" rules for all employees
2. One billing code for all employees
3. The same benefits and rates offered to all employees

With this approach, the user can input all of the information for a given employer on just one page within the system. This cannot be done with the second, employee-centric approach. With the second approach, building out even the simplest group will take going to a minimum of five pages. It's only an additional 45 seconds, but it's more.

Let's review this second, employee-centric approach. Under this approach, this is what you have:

1. Employees assigned to benefit subgroups
2. Employees assigned to timeframe (eligibility rule) subgroups
3. Employees assigned to billing code subgroups
4. Rates assigned to plans
5. Plans assigned to benefit subgroups

Now why would it ever be better to do things this way? Let's take a moderately complicated employer. This employer has the following:

1. Two sets of timeframes (eligibility) rules
2. Three sets of primary billing groups (divisions)
3. Six sets of secondary billing groups (departments)
4. Four sets of benefits groups (executives get more life insurance than other employees and some employees are paid biweekly and others semimonthly)

With the second, employee-centric approach, you will need to build out two timeframes subgroups + three primary billing subgroups + six secondary billing subgroups + four benefits subgroups = 15 subgroups.

With the first, benefit-centric approach, there would be 2 x 3 x 6 x 4 subgroups = 144 benefits subgroups. Yes, that is right, 144 benefits subgroups!

Let me tell you something about having 144 benefits subgroups. You never really feel confident that the system is correct. And when you have to change the system at next year's open enrollment—let's just say NIGHTMARE.

And this is what happened to us in our agency. We began having more and more clients that needed 50+ subgroups. This was in part because we were winning the trust of bigger employers, but it was also because we started to appreciate more the complexity of even our smaller groups as they insisted on having things reflected absolutely correctly in the system. As our smaller clients relied more on our system, for example, they wanted to use it to allocate benefits costs across different divisions and departments. As a result, the number of benefits subgroups they had multiplied.

Transitioning BerniePortal from being benefit-centric to employee-centric was awful. Imagine: We had to take all of these clients whose employees had logins already and condense their 50+ subgroups to five to ten. We had to do this without disrupting the client. The only time it was possible to do it was at open enrollment. We did it over the course of a year, running two parallel systems and parallel code bases that had to be maintained by our developers while we made the transition.

Ugh. Now imagine if we had already had thousands of brokers and employers using our system. If that had been the case, we simply would not have been able to make the migration from being benefit-centric to being employee-centric. We would have had to continue making "cloning" things easier and making auditing subgroups against each other more simple. No one would have been happy, but we would have muddled along. We know several products that serve the 1,000+ employee space that are in this position today.

To sum up, look for this. Ask about it. Here is the question:

If a client has a DOH provision for key hires and FOM 60 days for everyone else, offers more life insurance to execs than other employees, pays some employees biweekly and others semimonthly, and for billing purposes has three departments and six divisions, can you show me how that would be set up in your system?

You'll want to see 15 subgroups in that scenario. Two for eligibility rules, four for benefits, and nine for billing. If you see 144, run for the hills.

5 | How Many Ways Can You Fund Benefits?

How an employer funds benefits is a question that unleashes a large degree of creativity from brokers and their employer clients.

Basic employer contribution that varies with each plan and coverage tier. Defined contribution. Defined contribution, but only for ancillary coverages. Defined contribution with different buckets of employer money for different sets of benefits. Fixed percentage based on the "employee only" tier of a given "base plan." The ability to roll over employer money towards dependent coverage tiers because the employee chose a plan less expensive than the "base plan."

Accommodating all of these approaches and more is not easy for a benefits system. Part of the reason it is not easy is because of all of the different things that have to change about the basic functionality of the system for every single approach.

What do I mean? Let's review the impact of these variations on five areas that are basic functionality for any halfway decent benefits system:

1. Shopping cart totaling the employee's cost while they're electing benefits
2. Page at end of process summarizing the employee's cost
3. Login area where employee can always return to review elections and view information about the benefits he or she elected
4. PDF that is generated upon completing enrollment, summarizing elections
5. Reports that the employer or broker can pull

To explain how BerniePortal has to change to accommodate different funding strategies, I'll start with a chart outlining what BerniePortal sees as the major "forks in the road" for funding strategies and then screenshots from our system of just the "shopping cart" area that has to change when an employer is using defined contribution, but only for two buckets of ancillary coverage, versus not using defined contribution at all.

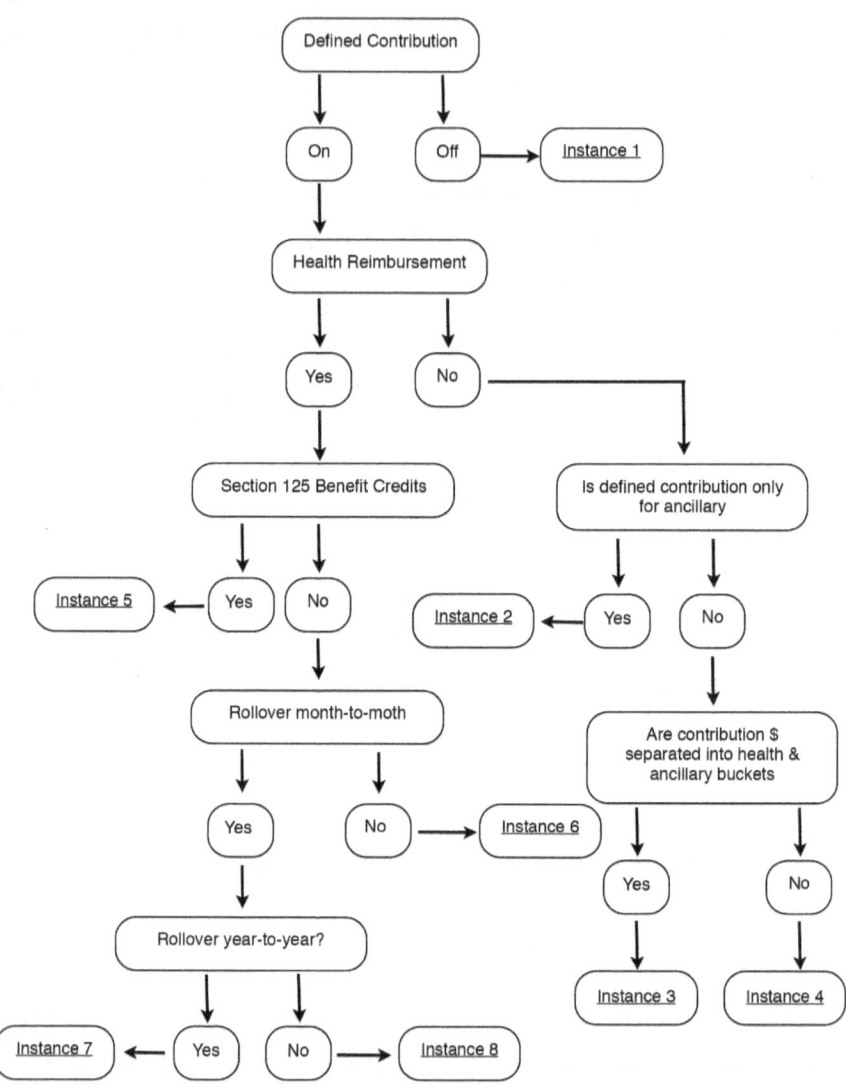

Using Defined Contribution

HEALTH COST: *(per pay period)*

Health	$200.00
Employer contribution	$100.00
Employee cost	$100.00

ANCILLARY COST: *(per pay period)*
BUCKET 1

Life	$7.75
Dental	$23.45
Vision	$5.80
Voluntary Life	$7.85
Short term disability	$0.00
Long term disability	$0.00
Total cost	**$44.85**
Employer contribution	$35.00
Employee Cost	$9.85

ANCILLARY COST: *(per pay period)*
BUCKET 2

Critical Illness	$0.00
FSA	$0.00
401(k)	$0.00
Total cost	**$0.00**
Employer contribution	$20.00
Remaining balance	$20.00

Total cost	**$244.85**
Employer contribution	$155.00
Employee Cost	$109.85

Not Using Defined Contribution

PER PAY PERIOD COST:

	Employee	Employer
Health	$100.00	$100.00
Dental	$0.00	$23.45
Vision	$5.80	$0.00
Life	$0.00	$7.75
Voluntary Life	$7.85	$0.00
Total cost	**$113.65**	**$131.20**

As you can see, it gets complicated. When you're selecting a system, ask to see how they handle this and whether the system can handle the funding approaches that you and your employer clients need.

6 | Integrations-
What Everyone Wants

"I need it to integrate." These five words are said by every healthcare broker and HR manager when discussing HR software. This is particularly true when it comes to the benefits component of their HR software. As a result, whether a system integrates and how it integrates is discussed on every single discovery call with every HR software vendor. Because the answer is complicated, the ensuing conversation often leaves no one satisfied. It's frustrating! Plus, given the billions of dollars pouring into HR software for small employers these days, it looks like there are only going to be more and more of these conversations. In this chapter, we'll cover in detail how this all works.

Let's start with the healthcare broker and HR manager's perspective on what it means to integrate.

Broker Bob explains to Developer David what "integration" means

When Broker Bob meets Developer David, he is thrilled. A real-life developer! Bob has been talking to all of these different vendors, none of which seem to understand the first thing about what it means to really integrate. But Bob has started wondering if the problem is that he is only talking to sales people, and not the guys who really do the work. Here is what Bob says:

> *David, so glad to meet you! Let me explain to you what I mean when I say we need integration in the HR software we supply our clients. Last year I was in Tahiti on vacation. I took a picture of my wife and I on the beach with my iPhone. Back home, when my housesitter turned on our Apple TV in our living room, the picture of us was right there on the screen! I know that because she sent me a message from her phone that popped right up on my Macbook Air and my iPhone at the same time. Boom! Integration. Now — is that how your software works as far as passing benefit elections to the insurance companies and payroll? An employee makes an election and — boom — the insurance companies all have the*

elections and the payroll company has the deduction? Oh, and by the way, I don't pay Apple a dime on an ongoing basis for all of the integration they give me — no per member per month for every member of my family or anything like that. What do you charge for your integrations?

Developer David has met people like Bob before. The truth is, Apple has set the bar so incredibly high, which is why it is among the most valuable companies in the world. David knows that for Bob to understand best how his HR software's integrations work, Bob will first have to understand a little bit about how software is built.

Well-built software platforms have three basic layers:

1. The data layer
2. The business layer
3. The presentation layer

Layers of Software	
1. Data Layer	Ultimately, "integration" is simply getting information from one "data layer" or database to another database
2. Business Layer	Where the subject matter logic is stored and answers the question: *"how is this thing supposed to work"*
3. Presentation Layer	Makes it easy to use and visually appealing

As you can see on the diagram, at a basic level two databases have to talk to each other to create an integration. When it comes to the average insurance carrier, they often have multiple databases. For example, one for eligibility and one for billing. This is very different from Apple, which has a single database from which all of your Apple devices pull. In other words, the experience Apple delivers in the story Bob shared is not an integration at all! When it comes to HR software and insurance companies, data needs to move from one database to another. That means an integration is required. As you can imagine, with multiple databases communicating between multiple companies, there is room for error. Again, Apple doesn't face this problem at all in the story Bob shared. Because different databases are generally configured differently, it is not so easy to just "turn on" an integration between two completely different companies and have data appear accurately in both systems. On top of that, the insurance industry isn't as technologically advanced as other industries. As a result, integration limitations are related to insurance company limitations, not HR software limitations. You might think "But companies like Zenefits were doing this, so it must be possible." The truth, however, is that Zenefits was never doing it. Zenefits just had a lot of money and employed a lot of people to do manual work to get data from its system into the carrier systems. As you can imagine, so much manual data entry is highly susceptible to errors.

Two approaches for moving data from one database to another

Now that we've defined "integration" as information moving from one database to another, let's look at the two approaches used in the industry for doing this.

1. Electronic Data Interchange (EDI)
2. Application Program Interface (API)

If you've talked to any HR software companies, you've probably heard the acronyms EDI and API thrown around. At a basic level, EDI and API are two approaches for transmitting data from one database to another. API is more advanced — some actually call APIs the EDIs of the 21st century. So what's the difference?

Let's start with Electronic Data Interchange, also known as EDIs. Good news — if you're familiar with file feeds then you already know what EDIs are. While EDIs are often seen as a step above faxing paper enrollment forms or manually inputting data into a carrier's website, they are tedious and still leave a lot of room for errors.

First, the files themselves are often times very difficult to interpret. Setting up an EDI file with a carrier can take months and carriers typically only integrate with companies with more than 100 employees. Furthermore, data is often only synced weekly, and certainly never in real time.

While EDI has drawbacks, due to pressures and circumstances in other parts of their businesses, file feed technology is the best integration that most insurance and payroll companies can offer. That said, some insurance, payroll, and other benefits-related organizations have made investments that allow them to do better. What is better?

> **"**
> Carriers typically only integrate with companies with more than 100 employees **"**

Better is an API integration, whereby the HR software is actually talking directly with the partner's system (rather than communicating via a file feed). API stands for Application Program Interface. Whether you know it or not, you interact with APIs every day on the web. Essentially, APIs are what makes it possible to move data between various databases in "real time," or instantaneously. Do you ever wonder how you can use your Facebook ID to log in to websites you've never been to before? You can thank APIs for that. How do APIs work, you ask? APIs are created by companies leaving parts of their databases "open" so other software platforms can easily integrate with them and request or send information.

You may be wondering how this relates to the insurance industry. APIs are capable of syncing with carriers whenever there is a change in benefits. Allstate Benefits is one of the only insurance companies in the country that is capable of this type of integration. That said, even they are only able to offer it for enrollments and qualifying events — terminations still require a file feed. It's important to note that while an API integration is better than file feeds, both are prone to issues. Any time multiple databases are exchanging information, errors can happen. Even Facebook has to have developers on its team dedicated to maintenance of the APIs that the company makes available.

We know what you're thinking — will there ever be a "single database" solution like what Apple has created, but for HR and benefits in the small employer space? There are two ways this could work. Let's review them both.

1. Carrier-centric approach: Carrier adds HR functionality to its platform

Let's take a look at what this would look like. With this approach, every carrier would have to build out HR functionality and offer all products. For example, Blue Cross Blue Shield would have to make functionality such as PTO tracking, onboarding, notices and reporting available as part of its software platform. This is very unlikely. It would take a significant investment in development and resources for carriers. It would also require believing that employers would feel comfortable turning all of their HR processes over to their insurance company. We are not aware of any carrier even trying to do this.

2. Employer-centric approach: Carriers rely more on HR platform databases

The more likely solution is the employer-centric approach. This would mean that carriers would rely more on HR platforms to hold the most up-to-date and accurate information when it comes to benefit elections. Worried that the employer-centric approach wouldn't be perfect?

It won't be. But even Apple has exceptions to its single database. For example, think about Apple's App Store. Apple has developed a set of standards and requirements for these apps, but there are still thousands of companies with apps and plenty of issues.

Similarly, with the employer-centric approach there are still going to be situations in which there just simply can't be a single database. For example, at the point of service, a doctor's office is still going to have to call the carrier to verify coverage. For this reason, in most instances the carrier will still need an eligibility database. Payroll is another example of where multiple databases will have to exist. However, payroll providers are already working to address the problems of multiple databases by developing open API. For example, ADP has created its own App Store similar to Apple's called the ADP Marketplace. ADP requires partners (software companies such as BerniePortal) to integrate via an API and meet specified requirements.

While the HR and benefits industry does not have anything approaching Apple's answer to the "integration problem" yet, it is headed in the right direction. When you are evaluating the different systems out there, ask them where they are in the journey of integrating with the insurance companies and payroll providers. Do they have any API integrations? Are they with payroll and insurance companies, or just one or the other? How do they charge for the integrations? Do they have any of their own API to make it easy for other parties to integrate with them? Do they have an iPhone and Android app, indicating the ability to make more API available in the near future? Are they doing billing for any carriers, thus moving towards an Apple-like solution to this integration problem for brokers and employers alike?

7 | **Licensing Model**

In the last two chapters we've talked a lot about the product. We'll do more of that in Chapter 9, but for now we're going to change gears and talk about the license you're being offered as an insurance agency. When it comes to a license, there are four categories of considerations you should make sure you understand.

1. Cost
   a. Flat fee license
   b. Minimum plus per employee per month license
   c. General agency provides license

2. Upfront training
   a. No training

b. Phone-based training

c. In-person training (sometimes optional, sometimes required)

3. Ongoing support
   a. Online knowledge base versus no online documentation
   b. Phone support for a subset versus all of your agency's employees
   c. Dedicated client services representative versus a general line
   d. Build-outs of employer clients done by the software company versus by you

4. Add-ons
   a. 1095-Cs: included or not?
   b. Onboarding, PTO, and other HR features: included or not?
   c. Integrations: included or not?

Let's review each of these categories in depth.

Cost

Most agencies will focus on this first. This is natural, as this represents hard dollars that will be coming out of your P&L. While long-term this expense should turn out to be a wonderful investment in your business that pays off in a big way, at first it will represent a hit to your income. It's also smart to evaluate the long-term impact if you are successful at moving the majority of your clients online.

With that in mind, the most attractive cost model is for an agency to be able to put all of its clients on a platform for one flat monthly or annual fee. In this model, an agency can pay $750 per month, for example, and move as many clients as it wants onto the system.

Another option on the market includes a "per employee per month" fee that starts with a minimum. For example, $2 per employee per month with a 1,000 employee minimum. In this scenario, the agency would start out paying $2,000 per month ($2 x 1,000 employee minimum) and then would begin to pay more than $2,000 once it added more than 1,000 employees to the system.

Finally, there are a few options on the market where you can get a license via one of the general agencies with which you work. In this model, you might not pay anything at all for the software. Long-term, though, if you believe that you need to incorporate online benefits into your value proposition (which you should), then you're going to want your own license and relationship directly with the software company.

Upfront training

How much training comes with the license is a big consideration. You can find options ranging from no upfront training at all to requiring that you fly somewhere for a few days of training.

When evaluating this aspect of the license, you should bear in mind that adopting online benefits technology is going to be transformative for your agency. Ultimately, it will change the way you do business. That change will represent huge improvements to the way you process renewals to how you manage adds and terms for your clients. To go into that with no upfront training time is likely only to work for agencies that are changing from one system to another (if it works at all). Certainly if you are adopting a system for the first time, the more training, the better. Bear in mind that a lot of training is going to be towards you figuring out with your team how work processes will change within your agency given the new improvements your system is going to offer you.

Ongoing support

This is another big consideration. How technologically savvy is your support team? Will they find some "hand-holding" to be beneficial as they get going on the new system? Could you use some extra back-office support when it comes to building out your employer clients during the busiest time of year? It's likely you'll find more support to be pretty beneficial versus less.

Add-ons

Finally, it's important to understand what is included in your license and what costs extra. For example, does the system do 1095-Cs? Do you have to pay extra for that, or is it included in the license? Is electronic reporting of the 1094-C and 1095-C data included or extra? How much? Is all the 1095-C work done by the software company, or do they third-party a portion of it to yet another vendor?

What about the other HR functionality? The system offers PTO tracking. Do you have to pay extra for it? If not, are you expected to support it? If there is an extra charge for it, can the employer pay it and, if they do, will the software company support PTO directly with the employer?

How about COBRA? Does the software company offer COBRA, or is it integrated with other COBRA vendors? How many? Does that cost extra?

Which brings up the other big category of add-ons: integrations. Ultimately, you and your clients will want your system to be integrated with the insurance and payroll companies. There is almost always some sort of add-on cost for these. For your clients that have fewer than 100 employees, bear in mind that this is largely going to be a moot point. The insurance companies, as a general rule, can't integrate below 100 employees. For your clients over 100 employees, make sure to ask how integrations will work. Does the software company do these in-house or outsource them to a third party? Is the software company integrated with any payroll companies? How do those integrations work?

You're going to want to know that the software company can do integrations. But bear in mind that you will rarely be integrating at the same time you are implementing your new benefits software with your clients. Just getting the software in place with your clients will be your primary focus for the first year after you've selected a system. Integrating will generally come after that with the majority of your clients who follow through with integrating.

A final note on the license model of the system you select

It can be easy to get lost in the weeds evaluating the above categories of considerations. You'll ultimately find that there are trade-offs among the categories. A system might be a little more expensive, but come with more training. Or it might have a flat fee cost model, but have per employee per month fees for carrier integrations when that comes into play for larger groups.

The bottom line is that you want to look for a licensing model that will allow you to implement affordably – but also successfully.

8 | The Company Itself

What about the company itself? You should certainly consider the dynamics at the company that you are selecting. Is it venture-backed? Owned by insurance companies? Is it associated with a general agency? Or maybe a different benefits brokerage? Is it cash flow positive or burning through money?

Venture-backed

Zenefits is the epitome of a venture-backed firm. It achieved fast growth quickly, fueled in large part the same way many brokerages grow – relationships. Its founder went through a class with other new small businesses in San Francisco, built relationships with his classmates, and ended up getting the AOR on their benefits packages. The fast growth Zenefits got via those relationships coupled with its location allowed it to raise a lot of money, fueling buzz and more growth from start-ups and other entrepreneurial businesses across the country.

A widely reported conversation between one of the venture capital backers of Zenefits and its founder is a signal of what to watch out for with a potential partner that is venture-backed.

The backdrop to this conversation was that Zenefits was going from $1 million in revenue to $10 million in just one year. The venture capitalist backing Zenefits, is reported to have responded to that news with the following:

"Why are you guys so f****** bush league? You should be at $20 million."

The founder did not stand up to his venture capitalist backer. The company proceeded to spend a lot of investor money in an effort to achieve a growth target that the venture capitalist – who had absolutely zero background or knowledge about health insurance or the business of advising employers on their benefits package – thought was correct.

The lesson for you? If you're evaluating a company that is venture-backed, ask about the venture capitalists who may really be the ones calling the shots. Are they going to push this company to grow faster than is possible, causing an implosion whose after-effects will impact your business as well? Or do they know insurance and benefits and understand that growth needs to be managed responsibly and sales growth cannot go beyond the systems and processes that the software company has in place to support?

Owned by insurance companies

If an insurance company or a group of insurance companies owns the firm you're evaluating, then you have an entirely different set of questions to ask.

Some of the questions are obvious. Do you have to offer that insurance company's products in order to use the software? Is the insurance company's name going to be on the software? Will other insurance companies avoid working with the software company because of the presence of the one that is an owner? In other words, if Acme Insurance is a big owner of the software company, will that make Beta Insurance reluctant to let you offer their products on it?

And then there is another set of questions. These revolve around the roadmap for product development. Is the insurance company setting the roadmap? Is that roadmap aimed towards solving problems for the insurance company, or solving problems for your agency or HR? Insurance companies have their own problems to solve, completely unrelated to what your employer clients or even your agency cares about. If you choose a product whose team is worrying too much about solving the insurance company's problems, you may find yourself with a product that is years behind a competitor who stays more focused on solving problems for employers and agencies.

As a result, you'll want to understand how the product development roadmap is set and who makes those decisions. If you see a lot of headlines about how the product is "powering" some facet of the insurance company's online systems or quoting engines, that can be a sign that the software company is designing for the insurer rather than for HR or for agencies.

Associated with a general agency

Just like with an insurance company, a general agency is a step away from the employer client. As a result, it will not have as sharp an understanding as you do of the challenges the employer has. It will be tempting for them to demand that the product roadmap disproportionately include solving the general agency's problems rather than the employer's problems. Eventually, this can mean that this company ends up with a less attractive feature set for your customers.

It can also be tempting for the general agency to limit the products that can be on their system to the products for which they are paid an override. You can see the internal meetings: Why would we let the broker put XYZ carrier on the system if we aren't being paid anything on it when they could just as easily use this other carrier on which we are paid overrides?

This does not mean that the general agency will do this – it just means you need to ask about it. If you're going to go this route, you need to get comfortable with the idea that the software firm is going to a) be as attentive to the needs of the employer clients you serve as you are and b) allow you to work with any carrier you want.

Associated with a benefits brokerage

The bottom line with this sort of firm: you need to know they are not going to go after your clients.

The primary advantage of this type of firm is that it should be just as in-tune as you are with the needs of the employer and the agency. After all, it hears more directly from employers just like you do and it has close knowledge on what it is like to be a broker living and dying by a possible

AOR change. It should also understand agency operations better than a general agency, insurance company, or venture capitalist possibly could.

And its product roadmap should be aligned with what you would want: solving for employer and agency needs. It should have a product lead today and that product leadership should extend as competitors who are associated with venture capital, insurance companies, or general agencies focus too much on needs outside of what the employer and agency need.

But that brings us up to the concern that this type of firm is going to end up calling on your clients – and trying to get the AOR for its own brokerage. One approach to this is to ask for what is called a non-solicit agreement alongside your license agreement that forbids the associated benefits brokerage from being able to call on any clients that you put on the software.

Beyond that legal protection, it is also worth evaluating the actual likelihood that this company's benefits firm is going to start calling on your clients. Is their benefits brokerage near you geographically? Are you in a market that would be easy for their brokerage to access? Does their brokerage believe in the idea of a call-center approach to benefits, or does it believe in the importance of a local advisor where there is a strong relationship between the advisor and the employer?

Cash flow positive

Finally, it is important to consider the financial strength of the firm. Imagine you sign an agreement and begin transitioning your clients and then they go out of business. It happens. Benefitbay is just one example. A company with a wonderful concept and wonderful team, it raised money, signed a big agreement with Humana, and got some traction with agencies nationwide. But they were never cash flow positive and were unable to continue raising money. They ended up having to close the business.

That was terrible for the individuals who poured so much into trying to make it successful. It was also terrible for the agencies and the brokers and service people who had poured money, time, and energy into learning about how their system worked or even moved clients onto their system only to have to move them somewhere else.

If you're talking to a firm whose salesperson makes a big deal about how they raised $2 million from a venture capitalist last year, keep in mind that venture capitalists expect eight out of ten of their investments to go out of business. In other words, raising venture money alone is by no means evidence of a sure thing.

At the same time, nothing in business or life is a sure thing. When you're gauging the strength of the software firm, ask them if they are cash flow positive or profitable. If not, when do they expect to be profitable? Do they have partners that signal strength? One pilot agreement with Humana was not enough to save Benefitbay. But if you see that they have agreements with multiple, big industry players that can be a good signal that they are financially strong and sticking around for the long haul. Even better if those agreements represent technology investments not just by the software firm, but by the industry player (e.g. insurance or payroll company). Also good if they have a long list of happy agencies that they can share as references.

9 | The Product Beyond Benefits, Plus a Note on Product Leadership

What does the product offer beyond benefits? Does the firm have product leadership? Is its leadership sustainable?

As a benefits broker, your long suit is advising on healthcare benefits. You know a lot about the transactional challenges related to offering and administering a benefits package. In fact, in most cases you know more about these challenges than your HR client does. That is part of why they hire you.

But as we discussed in Chapter 2, your HR client faces transactional challenges that stretch beyond benefits. They stretch beyond benefits, but they are also impacted by benefits – which is why it is important to understand how the software system you select handles them.

I'll pause here and share a story from back in 2012 about BerniePortal adding PTO administration to its set of available features. The benefits brokerage related to our firm, Bernard Health, had a 300-employee prospect that had an antiquated PTO tracking system provided by its current brokerage. To get the AOR, the broker had to provide a similar PTO system. I had a phone call with the prospect to understand their needs and concluded this wasn't that big of a deal and we would just add a PTO feature to BerniePortal. The employer made it sound like all we had to do was give someone 15 PTO days at the beginning of the year and then count down as the employee took them. No big deal. I committed we would get it done.

Ha! While PTO tracking is certainly less complicated than benefits, I eventually learned it still has a lot of "dark corners." I worked with one of our designers to draw how BerniePortal's new PTO feature would work based on my phone call with the prospect, and took the drawings to show the client. The barrage of questions came immediately. What about approvers? What about approvers being able to see a calendar of which employees were going to be out for a given period of days? What about accruing days? What about a waiting period before days started to accrue?

What about restoring days an employee requested off accidentally? What about requesting off past days because the employee forgot to request them through the system but had received verbal approval and now needed to mark that they had been taken? What about the side deals with certain employees who negotiated harder when they were hired and got 17 days per year instead of 15? And what about carrying over days from the prior year, but only up to a certain amount?

And then the big one – what about how in the world we were going to migrate current PTO data for 300 employees from their old system to the new system?

We got through it, and got a great PTO tracking feature as a result. And while I spent far more time on getting this PTO feature built than I thought I would, I learned a ton. I was also relieved to have the PTO learning chapter of my life behind me.

At least, I thought it was behind me. Then, the brokerage told another one of its clients about BerniePortal's great PTO feature. The client was eager to adopt it in place of what they had. I proudly did a demo for them and got a whole new set of questions. How do I set positive limits? Where do I set the accrual bank? What about negative limits?

Through that, I learned that there are multiple ways to configure PTO policies. We think we address all of them now, and we have clients using each of them happily, but there may be more in the future. We've also learned that each client needs hands-on help and support migrating from their old PTO tracking system to the new one.

I share this story to set up the following question you should ask when evaluating an online benefits technology firm: How do you handle the other transactional challenges our HR clients face?

We see online benefits firms taking one or a mix of three approaches:

1. Address directly, included in the broker license
2. Address directly, but outside the broker license
3. Don't address, but offer the ability to integrate with others who do

Let's evaluate each of these approaches, one by one.

First approach: address directly, included in the broker license

With this approach, the online benefits technology firm builds into its software the ability to do applicant tracking, onboarding, PTO tracking, time and attendance, compliance, and payroll – or some mix of these items – and then just makes it all available for the broker as part of its normal broker license. If the cost of the broker license is a flat monthly fee, this means the broker is getting the ability to give its clients PTO tracking for free, for example, as well as benefits administration.

The primary positive of this approach is obvious: It seems like it would be better to be able to offer more to your clients rather than less. If you can throw in PTO tracking with online benefits administration, even better than just benefit administration. Time and attendance on top of that? Sweet.

But do you know anything about the nuances of PTO tracking? Or time and attendance? Does anyone in your firm? Is it worth your time for your firm to build up a core competency in that area? Are your clients looking to their healthcare advisor to be their go-to for that sort of thing, or do they want you to stay focused on keeping up with the ever-evolving healthcare landscape?

The thing to keep in mind: if you give your clients a system to track PTO or time and attendance for free, they are going to expect you to support it. That means helping them think through how to transition from their old system in addition to helping to answer questions along the way.

If the software firm you selected gave these features to you for free as part of your license for online benefits administration, then all of that support is going to have to come from you. After all, the software firm won't be getting any additional revenue to help them provide any direct support to your employer clients for these other features. You or someone on your service team having to provide that support is the negative to this approach.

Second approach: address directly, but outside the broker license

With this approach, the software firm has built-in applicant tracking, onboarding, PTO tracking, etc. – but they are add-ons that the employer has the option to purchase. Of course, for a big or important enough client the broker can get them subsidized one way or another for the client just like it might subsidize other costs. But there is not a built-in assumption that the agency is going to have to support them.

Instead, the software company can support them more directly. The software company can help the employer think through how to transition from the old PTO system to the new one most effectively. The software company can answer questions along the way. Bottom line: The software company can support its own darn PTO feature while the benefits brokerage can focus on what it does best – advising the employer on how to manage its healthcare benefits package.

The negative of this approach is these additional features will cost. To the extent that you see supporting them costing your firm money because of the time you or your service people have to spend supporting them, this can end up being a wash or even to your benefit.

Third approach: don't address, but offer the ability to integrate with others who do

The final approach an online benefits technology firm can take is to ignore building any of the other features HR needs. Instead, this firm can work to integrate with other HR software firms who have products that address those needs. In certain circumstances, this approach can work exceptionally well.

The primary positive of this approach is that HR certainly won't be expecting you or your firm to support HR software that is completely different than the online benefits technology you've incorporated into your value proposition. One negative of this approach in general is that different software companies are going to have different agendas, different priorities, and thus different product roadmaps. Diverging interests among software companies all used by the same HR client can lead to an unhappy client through no fault of your own.

Another negative of the approach is that each company is going to have a separate sales and marketing budget that has to be covered by what it charges the employer. As a result, their fees will be higher than what an online benefits technology firm would have to charge if it had the other features available as add-ons. If your client finds itself paying a lot for HR features and could cut those costs by going with a broker who had selected a software firm that took either the first or second approach, it could put pressure on you.

Besides the transactional challenges your clients face beyond benefits, you as an agency face transactional challenges in your business that online benefits technology can address. As a result, you should also evaluate the product on what problems it solves for you and your agency.

What do I mean by this? The "end in mind" when you adopt a platform is that you will have the majority, if not all, of your clients using it one day. As a result, your clients' information will be in the system. Many systems have agency management capabilities that allow you, your brokers, and your service team members to be able to manage your clients more effectively. John Smith's wife called because she wants to know if John remembered to enroll the kids in the dental plan? Just a few clicks and you can tell her. Want to be able to see statistics on your book of business and compare? This can be a dashboard item in your broker view.

A note on product leadership

Product leaders offer products that are continuously rated over time as delivering superior value by their customers.

When evaluating online benefits technology, consider whether product leadership is important to you. How important is it to you and to your HR clients that the online benefits technology system you offer deliver superior value? In other words, that it provide more features that provide more benefits at a lower price than its competitors?

Additionally, how important is it that your partner be first-to-market with a given technology? Is it okay if your partner lags a year or two or more behind the product leader? Or is the nature of AORs such that you need to be able to offer the best each year?

If you decide that product leadership is important to you, the next step is to compare each product. You'll want to think first and foremost about the benefits feature. Does it do everything you and your clients need? What about integrations? Agency management?

As you are rating the products, ask the potential partners where they think they have product leadership and, if so, why they think it is important and sustainable. At BerniePortal, for example, we believe the fact that we came out of an agency that my brother, Brian, still leads gives us a tremendous advantage in this area. Why? We can incubate new features, carrier integrations, and payroll integrations before rolling out to our broker partners. Without that, we would have to be asking our broker partners to be the guinea pigs, which would invariably be much more problematic. Ask the other potential partners you talk to about their product leadership and I'm sure you'll get passionate answers from them, too. Ultimately, of course, you'll be the judge of who is most likely to continue to stay ahead of the curve.

The bottom line: Be deliberate about understanding each vendor's product roadmap, rating their products against the needs you and your clients have, and considering whether product leadership is important to you and who has it.

10 | Partners

Every online benefits platform wants to be integrated with all carriers and all payroll providers one day.

But these integrations take time. Besides the technology considerations, there is the people aspect. Most integrations in our industry require meetings, negotiating, working the project plan into the already-existing workload, etc. As a result, no system is integrated with everyone today.

When you evaluate the various systems, you should break down your questions about the system's partners into the following categories:

1. Health, dental, and vision carriers

2. Life and disability carriers
3. Worksite carriers (e.g. critical illness, cancer, accident)
4. Nontraditional (e.g. identity protection, prepaid legal, pet insurance)
5. Payroll companies
6. General agencies

Let's take these one at a time.

Health, dental, and vision carriers

On the integration side, all of these carriers are required to be able to accept the government-enforced HIPAA 834 file format for EDI purposes. As a result, if the software company you are considering has integrations with a lot of these types of carriers, it should be able to get a new integration set up with any of these carriers in relatively short order.

For example, if the company you're considering already has integrations with UnitedHealthcare, CIGNA, Anthem, a Delta Dental plan, Guardian, Superior Vision, and a couple of Blue Cross plans, then it should be relatively straightforward for them to get set up with the Blue Cross or Delta Dental plan in your state. Some companies even have a streamlined HIPAA 834 EDI engine within their benefits system that makes configuring for a new insurance company take a matter of hours rather than weeks.

Beyond integrations, some software companies may also be producing the bill for these insurance companies. In other words, instead of the insurance company sending the employer a bill based on the eligibility information it received from the benefits system, the bill is just produced by the benefits system itself.

Life and disability carriers

With these benefit types, you want to stay away from traditional "integrations" with the carriers.

Why? Because there is not a good standard governing how integrations work for these types of benefits. HIPAA 834 is sometimes forced on these benefits, but it does not work well. Furthermore, these carriers do not need eligibility information in the same way that the medical, dental, or vision carriers do. They don't need eligibility information because there are no doctors or other medical providers to whom they need to tell who has coverage and who does not. Any time there is a claim, the employer is involved in sharing that information with the carrier.

The bottom line for what this means is that, with these benefit types, it is natural and appropriate for the benefits system to be the sole keeper of eligibility information. This is similar to the self-accounting approach that larger employers have been taking to these types of benefits for years.

The other thing to watch for here is related to billing. Most small employers will not be comfortable with self-accounting. They'll still prefer to get a bill from the carrier. As a result, you'll want to see for which insurance companies the benefit system is capable of producing the monthly bill. Is it companies you work with today, or would you need to change? Are they in discussions to add the companies with which you already work?

Worksite carriers (e.g. critical illness, cancer, accident)

Most benefit brokerages have not introduced these benefit types to their clients to the extent possible. There are a variety of reasons for this. One is that these products can be incredibly complicated, which also makes them difficult for most systems to administer.

As things stand today, most of the carriers we see in this space are unable to integrate with online benefits systems in a way that will result in a happy small employer client and broker. One exception is Allstate Benefits, which with its real-time API integration can have its products appear to an employee in the same way that "core" benefits do.

This does not mean that a brokerage cannot work with other carriers. You absolutely can. The best approach, however, is most likely going to be to provide information in your system saying that these products are available, describing what they are, and then enrolling them outside of the system. Do "core enrollment" with your online benefits system and then enroll Colonial, for example, in Harmony. This is a perfectly acceptable solution that will yield a much happier client than trying to force these carriers' products into your core system. Wait to do that until these carriers have their own API capabilities.

Nontraditional (e.g. identity protection, prepaid legal, pet insurance)

Few groups in the 10 to 500 space offer these products today. Larger employers, however, do offer them and so have an edge when it comes to competing for new hires in that they have a more robust package. Leveling the playing field by helping your clients consider them is thus another opportunity.

Because these benefit types are relatively new and may not be subject to insurance rules and regulations, you should find that their technology capabilities are relatively strong.

How does this play into your platform selection? It is unlikely that you will begin offering these products to your clients in the same year that you implement the software with them. We'll talk more about that later, when we talk about how to implement in Part III. For now, you'll just want to know that the software companies you evaluate have these types of products in mind so that you will be able to offer them effectively in the future.

Payroll companies

Most of your clients are going to want the benefits system they use to "talk" to their payroll system.

Historically, the way this worked was via a spreadsheet upload from the benefits system to the payroll system. Increasingly, employers are finding this to be tedious and are insisting on real-time, API integration.

As things stand today, ADP is the only company that is capable of doing this. The other payroll companies, particularly Paycor and Paylocity, are working on catching up.

Because this functionality is so widely desired, many online benefits systems are opening up their own API to allow for faster time-to-integrate with more payroll companies. After all, there is an entire universe of independent, local payroll companies with loyal clients who are among your book of business.

When evaluating platforms, bear in mind that this functionality will be something your clients ask about and you'll want a partner that knows what it is doing in this area.

<u>General agencies</u>

Some brokers do not work with general agencies at all. Some work extensively with general agencies. If you work extensively with a given general agency, they probably already have a system that they sponsor in some way that they can show you. And you should absolutely consider using it.

Ultimately, you will want complete control over whatever benefits system you put your clients on and the ability to add whatever products you want – whether your GA has an override relationship with the carrier or not. As I've mentioned before, when evaluating your GA's system, make sure to have a handle on the answer to what extent your GA will support products on the system for which it does not receive an override.

Part 3:

How to Implement

11 | Implementing With Your Team

Once you've chosen a system, job #1 will be implementing it with your own team. Just like anything new that you try to introduce, you will have some colleagues who are more in favor of the change than others. Adopting an online benefits platform will prove to be transformational for your agency, but just like any change it will involve an exercise in change management by agency leadership.

The best first step is to buy a copy of the book "Who Moved My Cheese" by Spencer Johnson, M.D., for each member of your team. Ask them to read it and then hold a lunch or other session where you lead a discussion of it. The book has been celebrated as one of the best for getting teams ready for change. It uses a simple parable involving three mice to reveal important truths about how to deal with change more effectively. "More effectively" means you can implement change with less stress and more success. It is a short, simple read. If your whole team reads it, you'll find that they'll refer to it often during the adoption of your platform.

The next step is to train your team on the verbiage to use when things are not working with the benefits platform as expected. Specifically, these are the phrases you'll want your team to use when explaining a problem they're having:

1. I did _____.
2. I expected it to do _____.
3. Instead, it did _____.
4. I'm not sure why, can you help me understand?

For example: I clicked on "Start open enrollment." I expected to get a notification that employees could now enroll. Instead, it told me that I needed to confirm the employee benefit deductions for the "managers" subgroup. I'm not sure why it is telling me to do that, can you help me understand why?

To be clear, the above language is taking the place of the following:

1. The system doesn't work.
2. There is a bug.
3. There is a glitch.
4. I hate this thing.

In all likelihood, you're not going to pick a system that doesn't work. It is likely that whatever system you choose it will have many thousands of users and will have done many thousands of open enrollments. To say it doesn't work is likely not accurate.

It also makes the individual, his or her colleagues, and the team at the software company feel worse. Change is already stressful – if simply choosing different words to use to describe a problem can relieve some of that stress, then those different words should be chosen.

Even taking these steps – having your team read "Who Moved My Cheese" and adopting the best language possible to describe problems – might not be enough to manage your most frustrated colleagues. After all, some of your colleagues may be very used to doing things they way they have been doing them and don't want to change. You may have some individuals on your team whose desire to keep things the way they are is so strong they simply cannot keep their complaints to themselves. In the most egregious example I've ever seen of this, an agency leader had to kick her own service team member out of training because the individual was being so disruptive.

If you have someone like this on your team, it is necessary to have a direct conversation. This conversation should take place in a private, one-one setting. Following is suggested verbiage for that conversation. In this example, we'll call the difficult colleague "Kevin."

You: I've noticed that you've been very negative about implementing [name of system].

Kevin: Yes, well, given that I'm now going to have to support software in addition to insurance, there is a lot to be negative about.

You: I think you know this — but just to make sure — you know that the agency has gone to a lot of expense with this, right?

Kevin: Yes.

You: And you know that thousands of employers and employees use [name of system], right?

Kevin: Yes.

You: Do you think that we are going to cancel it?

Kevin: No.

You: Okay, so then what is the purpose of your negativity and complaining?

Kevin: [awkward silence]

You: There is not a purpose, and it is making this harder than it needs to be. Can you please stop?

Kevin: Okay.

This will be a difficult conversation, but not dealing with it will be more difficult in the long run. Also bear in mind that having this conversation once will likely not be enough. You'll want to follow up to praise Kevin when you see him handle a difficult situation related to the software in a positive manner, and also pull him aside and remind him in private if you see another demonstration of bad behavior.

Hopefully you won't have a "Kevin." Hopefully everyone on your team sees the need to make this transition to the same degree that you do and will be enthusiastic and pleasant about it!

That said, don't forget to ask when evaluating the different online benefit platforms to what degree they are going to support you and your team through this transition. Is there an opportunity for in-person training? Do you have an assigned account executive? What does the initial implementation look like? Getting off on the right foot with your own team is the best way to ensure that implementing with your clients will go as well as possible. Bear in mind that if your software company won't handle your team's questions, those questions are all going to come to you.

12 | Implementing With Clients

Successfully implementing your new online benefits software with current clients is critical to your long-term success. There is a right way to do it.

First, let's briefly review the wrong ways to do this for employers that are in the 10 to 500 employee segment. Keep in mind, I'm writing for the small employer segment right now. For larger employers, the approach would be different. Even as you get up to the larger end of 10-500 the approach may be different. This book, however, is about the small employer who makes up the majority of your book of business.

How not to do it

Do not have a luncheon or other seminar to talk about going online in general or about your new system in particular. Do not have a meeting with the client off-renewal to discuss going online or to do a demo preview of the system. Do not implement any other time than at renewal for the upcoming open enrollment.

What I just shared goes directly against what most brokers I've known think they should do to roll out the software. In other words, most brokers I've known think doing a seminar and having meetings to prepare for the transition is the best way to do it. I would probably think that if I were approaching it for the first time as well. After years of experience, though, I know that it is not the right way. I'll explain why you absolutely should not do it this way, but first let me explain how you should do it.

How to do it

First, do you have an agenda for your meetings with your clients? If not, now is the time to start having one. An agenda means that you've written out what you plan to cover with the client when you get together with them.

You should not bring up going online with your client until the meeting you have with them where you are going to present the health insurance renewal. Here is an example of what your agenda should look like for this meeting.

Benefits Renewal Meeting

1. Health renewal: 12 percent increase
   a. Other plan options with the same carrier
   b. Other carrier options
   c. Level funding options
   d. Other options considered
   e. What to charge employees

2. Dental renewal: 3 percent increase
   a. Other plan options
   b. Other carrier options
   c. What to charge employees

3. Vision renewal: flat
   a. Other plan options
   b. Other carrier options
   c. What to charge employees

4. Life renewal: flat
   a. Other plan options
   b. Other carrier options

5. New benefit option: Short term disability

6. Enrollment logistics
    a. Date / location for employee meetings
    b. [Name of online benefits system]
    c. Materials for meetings

In my experience, the first item on this agenda – the health renewal – will take up 90 percent of the length of the meeting. So if the meeting is booked for ninety minutes, it will take about eighty of them. The rest of the agenda is handled fairly quickly, and then it slows down again at enrollment logistics. Figuring out the dates and locations for the enrollment meetings can make the meeting run over if the client has to coordinate multiple different groups of employees.

By the time you get to item 6b, which, if you're doing this right, will just have the name of your online benefits system, everyone in the room will be ready to wrap things up. Here is what you say:

> *"Yes, great. Now let's talk about [Name of online benefits system]. This is an online benefits system our agency has adopted to make things easier for our clients and help them stay in compliance. We vetted the entire industry and selected this system and I'm confident you're going to love it. I just wanted to mention it today, we'll have it ready for your employees to enroll in conjunction with the enrollment meetings.*

Do you have any questions about this? If not, let's talk about materials – is there anything in particular you want me to make sure that we bring this year?"

Practice saying this with a colleague or in the mirror until you feel confident you can say it with poise and confidence. Even delivered with the most poise possible, it is likely that you will get some questions. Let's review the top two questions you're likely to get and how to handle them:

Q1. Wait – going online? I'm not sure my employees are ready for that. Can I see a demo of the system?

Yes, you can absolutely see a demo of the system. [Name of online benefits system] does a demo every single day. I will send you an email with information on how to attend. Note: you should make sure that your partner does daily demos. If not, then find out how often they do them and adjust accordingly.

Q2. You know, our employees are not very good with computers. I'd be concerned about telling them to enroll online.

You know, we've found that employees who are not good with computers also struggle with paperwork. We will be here to support employees who are not able to do it online, just like we would be here to support those who struggle with the paperwork. You're really going to find this to be much better.

Your answers should be short and succinct. Be comfortable in the silence that encompasses the room once you deliver your answers.

In that silence, a few things will be working in favor of moving forward with getting online. One of them is that you're likely to have the owner, CFO, or controller in the room. This individual likely only shows up for one benefits meeting per year – the meeting where the renewal is discussed. On balance, this individual is likely to be much more in favor of going online than HR or the office manager will be. He or she also outranks HR or the office manager. The combination of the owner being in the room combined with the owner's bias towards wanting to get things online will help make this a short conversation.

The other thing working in favor of moving online will be that everyone in the room will want this to be a short conversation. They will have just talked about benefits for 80+ minutes! They all have other things that need to get done, and they need this meeting wrapped up so that they can move on.

Once you've emerged from the meeting secure with the decision to move online, the pressure will be on to perform.

I realize that. But the pressure would be on to perform no matter what. To illustrate that, let's talk about what will happen if you try to implement utilizing a method different than the one I've described.

Giving more air to the conversation about going online

Whether you have a seminar, luncheon, or just schedule an off-renewal meeting with a client to discuss going online you're giving more air to the conversation. Giving more air to the conversation than necessary is not good for your clients and it is not good for you. Let's discuss why.

When you bring up to your clients that you have adopted an online system six months before renewal, some of your clients will naturally think of the brokers who have cold-called them in the past and talked about some system that they have. It will be natural for your clients to think "Hmmm, if my broker is going to want me to go online anyway, I might as well check out these other brokers and their system to make sure I get the right one for my company."

In other words, you'll be letting your competition in. Why would you do this?

Alternatively, some of your clients will think about other HR software they've seen ads for in the past. Or they'll think about their payroll company's benefits module. They'll ask you to help them compare those software options to your online benefits platform. I know one broker who found himself sitting through the demos of eight different HR software platforms for a client, some of which didn't even do benefits, as a result of giving too much air to the "going online" conversation with his client.

It's clear why this is not good for you. Why is it also bad for your client?

It is bad for your client first and foremost because your clients want a smooth open enrollment. Then, they want smooth processes for adds, changes, and terminations during the year. They rely on you for that. It is so easy when sitting through HR software demos to say "Oh, but wouldn't that one little feature that this system has be nice?" And then you're off on a tangent that distracts from the primary desire: a smooth open enrollment.

And as we discussed in Chapter 1, as a broker you can't reliably support more than one system. But your client doesn't realize or appreciate that because they don't know your business like you do. If your client goes and picks an alternative system, they are likely unaware they are putting their smooth open enrollment at risk.

Never forget: the same client for whom you bend over backwards to let pick their own system will blame you for any problems that occur during open enrollment.

In other words, the pressure is going to be on you no matter what. You know that – you're a broker, it has always been that way. The AOR can be a good thing, or a bad thing. Just like the pressure is on with everything else, it will be on with online benefits technology, too. Don't think that because you gave more air to the conversation about going online that your clients won't blame you if something goes wrong.

Given that you're going to be blamed no matter what and that the owners of your employer clients generally want to go online, giving the online conversation just the amount of air I've described here is the right amount. With the right leadership from you, your clients will move online. It won't be without hiccups – what open enrollment season doesn't have hiccups? – but it will be a transition everyone will ultimately be glad they made.

I'll close with one note about the employee open enrollment meetings. You've worked with your software partner to build out the system for your client, or maybe you've done it yourself. Everything is ready to go. The last step is to upload the census.

Stop. Don't do it.

Wait until after you've done the first open enrollment meeting. In fact, build into your processes and your slides for these meetings that your online system will be ready for employees to start enrolling two days after the first employee enrollment meeting.

There are a few reasons for this. One is that employers often make last-minute changes. Maybe it is to the employee deductions, or perhaps it is to add billing subgroup categories for cost allocation purposes. Or maybe it is because those street addresses that your client told you they couldn't get to you and so just upload the census anyway…well, now they have them and want to upload them. Regardless, no employer or employee is going to be upset that they can't go and enroll immediately after the first meeting. Here is verbiage you can use when explaining:

You'll be enrolling online this year in [name of online system]. To enroll go to [web address]. Your login information will be [explain login information]. Now, let's see, today is Monday. The system will be ready for you to login and make your elections on Wednesday and we want you to complete your elections by [date that you want to close open enrollment].

I promise you that no one will raise their hand and express anger that they can't go and enroll that minute, and you'll save yourself a lot of grief by doing it this way.

Now that we've reviewed how to implement with your current clients, let's review how to promote it with prospects.

13 | Promoting it to Prospects

When you meet with a prospect, you should take a questionnaire with you. This questionnaire should include a set of questions that you ask any prospective client. Once you have gone through the questionnaire with your client, you should explain that you have some ideas of improvements they can make. Then, ask if you can take what you've learned back, think about it, and return later with your recommendations. Done correctly, 90 percent of the time they'll agree to the follow up meeting.

What does this have to do with how to promote your online benefits system to clients? I want you to succeed. You cannot succeed at promoting your system if you are not following a process that allows you to get an understanding of how they are doing things before you give recommendations on how they should change.

Now let's talk about what should be on the questionnaire you go through in your first meeting with the prospect – what we'll call "Meeting 1".

Meeting 1 - The questionnaire

Your questionnaire should be divided into two sections. The first section should have questions about how they manage the transactional aspects of HR. The second section should ask about how they are strategically managing their benefits package.

When you sit down with the client in your first meeting, you should ask to start with brief introductions and then immediately ask if they are from whatever town seems most likely. So if you're in Bloomington, Indiana you would say "Great being here, do you mind if we start with brief introductions? Are you from Bloomington?"

The prospect will then give their background, at which point you should introduce yourself starting with where you're from. Your introduction should be no longer than their introduction, and no longer than about two minutes even if they took 10 minutes or more to introduce themselves.

Note: Sometimes in the introduction period, the prospect will begin talking about their benefits package. I've seen prospects talk for 30 minutes, prompted only with "So are you originally from Nashville?" When they do that, immediately take out your questionnaire and begin filling in responses to the questions they are already answering.

Once introductions are done, say the following:

*Okay, great. Now as you know, healthcare benefits have become more and more complex and impact almost every HR system these days. I have some questions that first cover how [prospective employer name] handles the **transactional** challenges of HR, and then some questions about how it handles the **strategic** side of offering benefits.*

Your questionnaire should be visible to the prospect when you say this. When you finish saying it, immediately ask the very first question at the top of the transactional section. It should have to do with asking how they go about recruiting new employees to join the company. Do they use a job board, how do they share feedback among various hiring managers or influencers, etc.?

The prospect might ask at various points "Why do you need to know that?" You should have a ready answer each time. After asking twice and you having a ready answer twice, the prospect will conclude you know what you're doing and stop asking.

What would the ready answer be to questions about their recruiting process?

Well, some employers appreciate being able to more easily show their benefits package to prospective employees. If that is the case here, we have some tools that help make that easier. But we can move on – let's talk about onboarding a new hire. How does that individual fill out the W-4 and I-9 and then also get information about the benefits package?

Once you are through the section that asks about how they manage the transactional challenges of HR, move to the section that asks about the strategic side of their benefits package.

Here you should ask everything you would need to know if you were already their broker. What benefits do they offer? What coverage tiers? What does the insurance company charge them for each coverage tier? What do they contribute as an employer to the cost of coverage for each coverage tier? Who manages COBRA? How many deductions do they have per year? And so on.

Some of you reading may be thinking "Ask them the rates? Are you crazy? They'll never tell me what the insurance company is charging them!"

Yes, they will. They absolutely will. If they refuse to give you the rates they are being charged, ask why. They will say something like the following: "Well, if I tell you what I am being charged then when you go run quotes you'll just barely get underneath those rates."

At that point, you should bring out the printed agenda you had made for this meeting. (Note: You should have an agenda for any meeting you have with anyone. This one will be the same for every prospect you meet with, except the title at the top will be customized with the prospect's name).

The agenda should call the meeting you are in "Meeting 1." It should explain that this meeting is to get an understanding of their situation. Then, in "Meeting 2," you give recommendations based on what you learned in "Meeting 1." Those recommendations can only be as good and precise as the information you get in "Meeting 1." By all means, you can use ballpark numbers when formulating the analysis that you present in "Meeting 2," but if they go ahead and give you their rates they're going to get a more precise analysis.

Another thing they may say is that they may claim that they don't have the rates. At that point, you can point out that the rates are on the monthly invoice that they get from the carrier, and ask if they have a copy of a recent invoice. If they say that they don't have it handy, smile, be pleasant, and say you're happy to wait and then just sit there quietly. More than nine times out of ten you can get this information.

Again, you might be thinking – what in the world does this have to do with presenting my online benefits system? The point is that you'll be most successful if you fold your online benefits system into your overall value proposition. That includes how you present it alongside what you're recommending a prospect do with their benefits package.

Before we move on to what to do in Meeting 2, I want to emphasize one point. At no point in Meeting 1 should you talk about any aspect of your value proposition, including your online benefits system.

For example, if they say:

> *Oh my dear God, our open enrollment process is such a mess. We have 180 computer scientists in 35 offices across the country and right now we're faxing them the enrollment forms and then they are faxing them back. We had 15 of our computer scientists quit after open*

*enrollment last year – each one saying that they found
HR to be out of touch and that benefits should be online.*

Your response should be:

*Oh no, that's terrible. I might have some ideas about that.
It sounds like open enrollment is all done with paper. Is
the same true for adds / changes / terms during the year?*

And then just keep going through your questionnaire. Do
not, under any circumstances, start talking about how
you can solve their problems. This is not the time for that.
Meeting 2 is the time for that. If they directly ask you "Do
you have an online benefits platform that we can use?"
then you should say "Yes, and we'll definitely talk more
about that. For now (and then kind of lift up or motion to
your questionnaire) I've got a few more things I want to
make sure I understand."

Part of the reason for this is psychological. In many cases,
a prospect's guard will be up in Meeting 1 and they'll
shoot down anything you say you have that could solve
a problem that they have. They'll be much more open to
hearing about your solutions if you let this meeting be you
learning about them. Give them air to tell you all about
what they're doing. Then, they'll reciprocate for you in
"Meeting 2" by giving you an opportunity to share your
recommendations with them.

Meeting 2 – The presentation

Okay, so you've gathered all of the information you need for your questionnaire and you've scheduled a follow up meeting with the prospect. Now it is time to put together the presentation and recommendations you'll share in the "Meeting 2."

Your presentation and recommendation should be divided into two sections. In the first section, you'll share how the transactional challenges of HR are best solved with software and you have software that will allow them to manage those challenges more effectively. In the second section, you'll share how the strategic challenges of offering healthcare benefits are best managed with a smart, experienced, strategic problem-solver. You are that smart, experienced, strategic problem-solver and you'll illustrate that with the great recommendations you'll share on what they can be doing that they are not right now.

Before you do any of that, though, the first few slides of your presentation should play back to them some of the key insights you learned from them during your "Meeting 1." The title of these slides should be "Meeting 1 Takeaways." You should have a lot of detail here. This is in part to help them remember that they told you all that stuff, and to illustrate that you were listening. But you'll also want to be absolutely sure to include pain points they said that they had in the first meeting that you know you can solve.

Example: If they said that they enroll with paper and it's a mess and they want to be online, you should simply have on the slide that they said that. It is not necessary to talk a lot on these "Meeting 1 Takeaway" slides. You can simply have them up on the screen. Everyone can sit in silence and read them, and you can simply ask "Did I get these things right?" They'll say yes, and then you can get into the meat of your presentation. Each time your presentation addresses one of the pain points that they had said they had, you should tie the two things together for them explicitly: "You said in Meeting 1 that you needed to get online, and I've been using this system with my clients successfully and know you'll like it as much as they do."

The "Transactional Challenges of HR" section will largely be the same from prospect to prospect. You'll have screenshots of your online benefits system, and explain how it takes the paper pain out of open enrollment as well as adds, changes, and terms during the year. If they mentioned a specific pain point, you'll want to make sure to have a slide that directly addresses that pain point. If there is a pain point they mentioned related to another part of the HR ecosystem that your system helps to address, be sure to mention that as well.

The "Strategic Challenges of Healthcare Benefits" section will probably not be exactly the same from prospect to prospect, but it will likely rhyme. If you are big on HRAs, you should have a few slides analyzing what HRAs would do for the prospect. If you're big on level funding, then that might be it. Or it could be self-insuring, or HSAs, or defined contribution. Or maybe you're equally comfortable with an array of approaches and you give them an idea of how each would work for them, based on the numbers they gave you in the first meeting.

At the end of the meeting, the expectation should be that they are going to sign an AOR making you their new broker. The best way to do this is to establish with the agenda you share in the Meeting 1 that they will have all of the information they need to know whether to hire you or not at the end of the Meeting 2. Then, have the AOR prepared so that you can leave it with them at the Meeting 2.

I'll close this chapter with answers to some anticipated FAQs.

Q1. But what about a demo? Won't they want a demo of the system?

It is possible that they will say that they want a demo. If they do, then you should encourage them to attend the daily demo that your software company does and you should follow up with them with the details for that demo. (Remember, not all software companies do a daily demo. You should ask about this when you are evaluating the various online benefit platforms if you think it could be important to you).

Most prospects will not follow through on attending a demo. They'll like that one was available, kind of like they like that you have references. But they won't follow through on attending the demo (just like a lot of them never call references). From our experience, whether a prospect attends a demo has no bearing on whether they hire you or not. They want a smooth open enrollment. If you're going to be their new broker, they should trust you when you say that your platform will deliver it. We think most employers know this intuitively, which is why so few of them actually follow through on attending the demo.

Q2. But wouldn't it be stronger if I did a personalized demo for them on-site?

No, absolutely not. If you think a personalized demo is the key to landing a new prospect, the way to do it is to set up a meeting with the client where you are physically sitting with them in their office or conference room. Then, whoever is going to do the personalized demo (it may be someone from the software company helping you out or one of your own people) should do the demo via a webinar. Any personalized demo should only be done after the prospect has attended a general demo and they should have supplied specific questions they have about the software in advance.

It is important that it be done this way. You sitting next to your client viewing the demo with him or her will allow you to observe physical cues that he or she is not happy with something or has additional questions that are not being answered. It is also unlikely, especially at first, that you'll know everything there is to know about the software and so having someone from the software company do this type of demo for you via webinar is best. After the webinar is over, HR will often have other questions that you'll be able to address right then and there or you'll be able to write down and follow back up on. It will also be a natural opportunity for you to go ahead and ask for the business or ask what more they need to see in order to feel comfortable hiring you.

Q3. Bring the AOR to the meeting?? Isn't that coming on a little too strong?

It is all in how you present it. If your demeanor is laid back and you present this as simply the next step, you'll be fine. The agenda is really important. Here is a sample of the kind of agenda I've been referring to:

[Name of employer prospect]

Agenda

[Date]

1. Meeting 1
    a. Understanding management of transactional HR challenges
    b. Understanding management of strategic benefit challenges

2. Analysis/formulation of recommendations

3. Meeting 2
    a. Presentation of recommendations
    b. Decision: move forward this year, or decide to stay in touch

Present the AOR simply as what it means to make a decision to move forward. Also be amicable about the fact that the decision may be just to stay in touch.

Q4. What if there isn't time for two meetings? Say their renewal is January 1st and it is already December 7th – what then?

In our experience, there is always time for two meetings. Don't short-circuit your sales process just because the renewal date is coming up soon. In this example, you may meet on December 7th to gather the information and then again on December 8th to present. In desperate enough situations, this can work even with groups that have hundreds of employees.

Remember – the information you gather in Meeting 1 is information you're going to need if you're the new broker anyway. Is it possible you won't get the client this year because you're meeting too close the renewal? Yes, absolutely. But that is true whether you follow the sales process or not.

In other words, if you go in and simply pitch them on December 7, you're equally likely not to get the client because you're too close to the renewal. What is worse, though, is that you'll also create a much worse impression than if you follow your process and just ask questions in Meeting 1. The broker who focused on asking questions in Meeting 1 is going to get asked back at some point, because the employer is going to want to know what the recommendations were going to be.

14 | Impact on the Bottom Line for Your Agency

Most brokers intuitively understand that adding an online benefits platform will help them in four concrete ways:

1. Retain clients
2. Gain new clients
3. Generate agency efficiencies translating to cost savings
4. Help them help their clients add lines of coverage

Some of you will win the trust and AOR from one or more several hundred-life groups with the system you select. Maybe you'll send an email to your software partner like this one that I received earlier this year from one of BerniePortal's licensees in California:

Hello Alex,

I just wanted to let you know we BOR'd a 400 life group today thanks in part to a couple of great Portal demos. We are still pinching ourselves.

Thanks to everyone on your team for the responsiveness and professionalism!

Those wins will be sweet and will generate significant ROI for you in relation to your investment in your online platform.

But in this chapter we're going to focus on your current book of business. It is easy to see how your online platform will help you get new clients. In many ways, however, the key to getting the most out of your platform is implementing it with current clients.

Here is why this is so critically important for you:

1. Your clients, on average, are not offering robust benefit packages.
2. The challenges that prevent them from offering robust benefit packages are addressed by being online.
3. This means that if you can help your clients get online, then they will expand their benefit packages.

4. When your clients expand their benefit packages, you will get more commission revenue on the same book of business.

5. More commission revenue from the same book of business means you'll have a much more profitable business.

6. This means more money for you while you're running your business.

7. It also means a much higher sales price should you ever decide to sell it.

Let's talk about Point #2 – the fact that the challenges that prevent an employer from offering more robust benefit packages are addressed by being online.

Large Employer Health Benefits Package

1. Health
2. Dental
3. Vision
4. Life
5. Voluntary Life
6. Long term disability
7. Short term disability
8. Critical Illness
9. Cancer
10. Accident
11. Telemedicine
12. Legal Shield
13. Identity Theft
14. Pet Insurance

Your average small employer is only offering these benefits

This is true even though they are competing for many of the same employees as the large employers

What are the key challenges preventing an employer from offering a more robust benefit package?

Some of you are thinking hard dollar cost. The average small employer does not want to pay more money for benefits. But that is not it – most of the additional benefits can be offered at no hard dollar cost for the employer. Instead, it is the *transactional costs* related to offering more benefits that is preventing your employers from expanding their benefit packages.

When the idea of offering more lines of benefits comes up, your employer clients are thinking about the additional paperwork, the additional payroll deductions that will have to be entered in payroll, the additional bills they will have to pay and to audit. Transactional costs even prevent you from wanting your clients to offer more benefits – explaining guaranteed issue rules for voluntary life, or having unmet participation requirements when offering voluntary short term disability. These sorts of things represent transactional costs to you and, if the group is not big enough, can even prevent you from wanting to offer more benefits.

Being online addresses these transactional costs. The online benefits platform gets rid of the need for paperwork for all of these additional benefits. It collects payroll deductions all in one place. It can even sync to payroll.

Bills can come from one place in the benefit system – and are always right because HR can correct them in real time. Many carriers will waive participation requirements when an online system is being used and the system will handle explaining guaranteed issue and distributing the EOI for people who go over.

In other words, once your clients are online, challenges related to expanding the benefit package melt away. Because your small employer clients compete with large employers for many of the same talented employees in the marketplace, they'll ultimately want to offer benefit packages that are just as robust.

Large Employer Health Benefits Package

1. Health
2. Dental
3. Vision
4. Life

Your average small employer is only offering these benefits

5. Voluntary Life
6. Long term disability
7. Short term disability
8. Critical Illness
9. Cancer
10. Accident
11. Telemedicine
12. Legal Shield
13. Identity Theft
14. Pet Insurance

What if they were competing with large employers more effectively by offering all of these benefits?

You already know this, but I'll say it anyway. As your clients add these additional benefits so that they can compete more effectively with larger employers in the war for talent, you'll gain commission revenue every step of the way. It is a situation where everyone wins. Employees get more options, the employer has a more robust benefit package to help it compete more effectively, and you get additional revenue.

The next question is how much more revenue. Let's put some numbers to it.

Line of Coverage	Estimated PEPM Commission
Voluntary Life	$1.25
Long term disability	$1.50
Short term disability	$2.00
Critical illness	$10.50 / $1.50
Cancer	$10.50 / $1.50
Accident	$7.75 / $1.25
Telemedicine	$0.50
Legal Shield	$0.50
Identity Theft	$0.50
Pet Insurance	$0.50

- 15% - 30% revenue growth
- 70%+ margins → 2x profits
- All while helping clients improve their benefits packages and helping employees get coverage they otherwise could not.

Now let's apply the above chart to your book of business.

Say that your book of business is generating commission revenue of $1 million and that the profit margin is 20 percent, or $200,000.

If by helping your clients get online and then grow their benefits package you can generate 15 percent to 30 percent revenue growth, that means that same client base can be generating $1,150,000 to $1,300,000 in revenue for your agency.

This additional revenue will carry a very high profit margin because these are clients who you are already servicing. It is unlikely you will need to hire a single additional service team member as a result of adding this revenue.

As a result, your book of business will now be generating profits of between $350,000 and $500,000 instead of profits of $200,000. If you have a $2 million book of business, then just double the numbers in the example. If you have a $3 million book, then triple them. If you have a $4 million book – you get the idea.

Furthermore, at some point in the future you may want to sell your book of business. These sales transactions are often done at a multiple of revenue, and the multiple is impacted by how profitable the book is. In other words, the more profitable you can make your book, the more you will be paid if you sell it one day. So by expanding profitability you'll get paid many times over – every year that you enjoy that increased profitability, and then in a big way the day you sell.

So while it is always exciting to get a new client like the broker in California who emailed me after getting the 400 life group with BerniePortal, don't lose sight of the massive opportunity with your current clients. You'll be helping them, their employees, and also your own agency.

On that note, I'll close. I am so glad to be part of this industry. Truly, I cherish the many relationships I've made while working in it and I relish the constant change and personal nature of the work. Whether you ultimately choose my company's platform, BerniePortal, as the right one for your agency or not, I hope that the experiences I've shared in this book are helpful to you in your online benefits journey!

Appendix

<table>
<tr><td rowspan="2">Appendix 1</td><td>How P&C Agencies Can Use a</td></tr>
<tr><td>Platform to Expand into Benefits</td></tr>
</table>

Insurance agencies that historically focused on property & casualty have a once-in-a-lifetime window of opportunity to expand into benefits in a really meaningful way. The opportunity is related to benefits technology, and the best agency leaders are taking advantage.

The window is that most employers aren't yet handling benefits and HR online, but increasingly want to be. P&C agencies have never had trouble landing meetings, but have had trouble having a clear differentiator over other benefits brokerages. Right now, before the window closes and every employer is already online, benefits technology can be that differentiator.

Once you get a meeting with an existing client, you can set your agency apart as more than just benefit experts, but as providing solutions to the transactional challenges addressed in Chapters 2 and 3.

Case Study

Ieuter Insurance Group is a full service agency that has served the Greater Lakes Bay Region for over sixty years. While being a well established agency, it was not capitalizing on its share of the benefits market.

The agency was introduced to benefits administration platforms at a conference and knew technology was the solution to growing its group benefits division. After returning from the conference, Ieuter Insurance Group began to research platforms.

Erika Garrison, Employee Benefits Specialist at Ieuter Insurance Group shares, "As far as we know, we are the only agency in Midland that offers a benefits administration platform. We are a young department and we are always looking for ways to differentiate ourselves."

Ieuter Insurance Group is one of many P&C agencies recognizing the value in differentiating themselves with an online benefits administration platform.

A look at the numbers

Let's say you set a meeting with 75 groups with 50 employees each and an average commission of $30 per employee per month. If you're able to close 20 percent of those meetings and gain 15 new clients, that represents annualized revenue of $270,000 per year.

Further, that is just with a 20 percent close ratio. We have seen agencies report close ratios as high as 31 percent, which in this example would result in new client annualized revenue of over $418,500 per year.

The biggest challenge most agencies have after adopting the right HR/benefits system is getting enough meetings with prospects. For agencies that have a P&C arm that is much larger than the benefits side of the house, getting in front of potential clients will not represent as much of a challenge.

But once in front of the prospect, all agencies need a deal-winner. Right now, benefits technology can be it. But as the industry as a whole moves online, that window will close. When the majority of agencies are offering a benefits administration and HR platform, having a software solution will become a deal-qualifier—in other words, a requirement to get a seat at the table, but not necessarily enough to win.

Once you've decided to adopt the approach that is working for agencies like Ieuter, you need to pick a platform, hire a benefits person if you don't already have someone, and then help them set meetings and close. Let's review each of these steps in-depth.

Step 1: Pick a platform

There are a handful of benefits platforms that have emerged as market leaders, and all of them will provide an online benefits enrollment experience. But when comparing benefits and HR software vendors, there are a few other factors you will want to consider. Use this book to help you identify the right platform for you.

Step 2: Hire someone who is tech-savvy and interested in healthcare

When you hear "tech-savvy," you might immediately think of hiring a Millennial or recent graduate. But this doesn't have to be a young person, it just needs to be someone confident enough with technology to become trained on your new platform and assist the agency in going online.

This person will also need to be trained on how to sell and position the software with prospects, which is where a tested method for revenue growth from the benefits platform will come especially in handy. An effective go-to-market strategy is necessary for using the platform to win new business.

Next, this person will need to meet with the carriers in your market. If you already have someone on your team who does group benefits, you may already have these relationships.

Step 3: Set meetings for them and help them close

This is where you can leverage your existing P&C relationships to win new business.

You will be shocked how much of the meetings will revolve around how the software will make HR's life easier. If you have a P&C client whose broker is not currently offering them any sort of tech tool, you having a solution for benefits administration, onboarding, compliance, PTO and more will be a clear differentiator.

This can result in significant revenue growth for your agency. While the window of opportunity is still open, P&C agencies are uniquely qualified to leverage their existing books of business to capitalize on benefits technology as a deal-winning solution and service.

Appendix 2 | A Deep Dive into EDI

Because EDI is the kind of integration brokers are most likely to encounter, it is worth having a working knowledge of how it works "on the ground." This overview of the steps for getting an EDI feed set up are just what you need.

Step 1: Mapping the carrier's "Companion Guide"

To understand EDI, one must first understand HIPAA 834. This is the benefit industry's "standard" format for communicating eligibility electronically. The HIPAA 834 was born out of the Workgroup for Electronic Data Interchange, which was created by the Secretary of Health and Human Services in 1991. This group issued industry recommendations for carriers and partners to adopt standardized EDI formats. The recommendations became part of HIPAA, which passed in 1996, and final "standards" were released in 2000.

"Standard" is in quotes because each carrier handles HIPAA 834 a little differently. In other words, the way carriers handle HIPAA 834 certainly "rhymes" from one carrier to the next, but by no means is it the exact same song every time.

When you tell a carrier that you want to do EDI for an employer, the first thing they will send you is their "Companion Guide." Sticking with the musical analogy, the "Companion Guide" is like sheet music, explaining that carrier's version of HIPAA 834.

In the Companion Guide are segments. Segments are like the musical notes or building blocks on which HIPAA 834 is constructed. The HIPAA 834 file makes available a wide variety of different segments.

This is how it works in BerniePortal. Other platforms may use an Access Database, or other means.

Some of these segments are used by almost every single carrier. They often appear in the same order from one carrier to the next. It is common to see that a given segment holds the same type of eligibility data from one carrier to the next.

For example, the "N3" and N4" segments are almost always street address and city, state and zip code, respectively. Other segments are often the same from carrier to carrier.

But not always. There aren't hard and fast rules about what segments a carrier uses, what order it requires they appear, or what type of eligibility data they hold.

One carrier could use the H34 segment to hold a certain type of data and require it to be the fifth segment to appear. Another carrier might require that the H34 segment hold a totally different type of data, and require it be the seventh segment to appear.

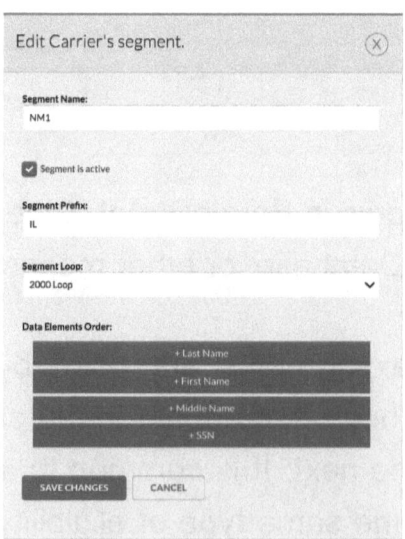

This brings us to the following terms: used, order, eligibility data. These terms are the key to unlocking the puzzle of how a carrier's HIPAA 834 song goes.

1. Which segments does the carrier <u>use</u>?
2. In what <u>order</u> does the carrier require them to appear?
3. What <u>eligibility data</u> does the carrier require to be in that segment?

Answering those questions correctly is the key to mapping an EDI feed for a carrier. It's what the carrier's Companion Guide is designed to tell you. If you like puzzles, you may even enjoy this aspect of EDI. One great thing about this step is that once you have the mapping correct for a given carrier, you'll never have to map for that carrier again. No carrier is going to change its version of HIPAA 834. Because so many groups are using its version, trying to change would be a nightmare.

Step two: Creating the HIPAA 834 file

Once you map the carrier, you will pull eligibility data for clients that you have set up with the carrier. You will work with your carrier partner to determine whether you will pull the eligibility for these employers all in one file, one group per file, or a selection of groups per file.

Step three: Submitting the file to the carrier

Every carrier has its own process for accepting HIPAA 834 files. Here are just a few of the options you may see.

1. Some can accept a file that has multiple groups on it.
2. Some need one group per file.
3. For others, it depends on a variety of factors.
4. Some require submission to a SFTP (Secure File Transfer Protocol) site.
5. Some allow for email submission.
6. Some require one test file before going to production.
7. Some require multiple rounds of testing.

At this step, you will be working collaboratively with your carrier partner to take the above steps that the carrier needs in order to go live with EDI for your employer client. Once you are live, you will submit these files on an agreed-upon schedule with the carrier, typically weekly.

One thing to bear in mind: Unlike the mapping in Step 1, you are never really done with submitting files to the carrier. Most carriers will require going through the testing steps before "going live" with every group you add to EDI, and also at each group's renewal.

Step four: Error reports

Each week, the carrier will send you an "error report" with any discrepancies it found between its database and the EDI file you sent them that week. Your team will work with your carrier partner to resolve the discrepancies as appropriate.

The two most common types of discrepancies are demographic and coverage-related. Every week, you are sending the entire group's eligibility information to the carrier through the file feed. If an employee changed their address, for example, or typed a different social security number than what the carrier has on file, it will flag as a mismatch.

Coverage-related discrepancies could involve a termed employee, for which you might need to verify the end date of the employee's coverage. Another example is a dependent who has aged off the employee's plan. In these cases, the broker might work as an intermediary between the employer and the carrier to verify the correct information.

Error reports are often spreadsheets, but can also be PDF files or emails. You'll generally receive these every week.

In both demographic and coverage-related cases, the broker generally needs to confirm any changes or correct any inaccuracies with the carrier before the next file is sent the following week.

How will these discrepancies be resolved? When you set up an EDI feed with a carrier, they will ask you to designate a discrepancy contact at the beginning of the process. This person will receive the error report after submitting the file and will work with the carrier to resolve any issues. In many cases, the broker can log on to the group's account on the benefits administration platform to review updated information and communicate changes to the carrier.

Very hands-on brokers may be aware of coverage-related changes before they receive any error reports. Others may not have that level of detail. Regardless, it is important not to ignore these reports. Missing a big error can cause a lot of billing and even coverage issues.

If this all sounds complicated, that is because it is. Having a high-level, working knowledge of how it works can help you navigate the integration waters with your clients.

Acknowledgements

I'd like to thank the entire BerniePortal and Bernard Health team for help with this book. None of this would exist without my brother Brian, who leads the health insurance agency from which BerniePortal was created. His team's insights, along with our other broker partners, inform so much of what we do.

I'd also like to specifically thank Sarah Weinstein, who leads our marketing team's efforts and oversaw this project from beginning to end. Several members of that team also made big contributions — Emily Kubis with the manuscript and Kati Fredericksen, who is responsible for all of the wonderful illustrations throughout.

I'd also like to thank my wife, Erin, and entire family for all of their support both in this project and life in general. Thank you!

There are many in the healthcare and technology industries that have been so helpful to me along the way. John Cary at Blue Cross Blue Shield of Tennessee helped me get a contract in 2006 when I had just passed the licensing test and taught me a lot of what it means to be a broker. Kevin Thompson at Humana and others at other carriers provided similar help. Andy Vetor, now Executive Vice President over benefits at MJ Insurance in Indianapolis, was also instrumental in helping me learn the industry. I'll never forget the day Andy explained to me what an "AOR" was. Rhonda Marcucci's insights at Gruppo Marcucci have been invaluable along the path of building BerniePortal. While I've never met him, Joel Spolsky taught me so much about building software and just the business of software in general through his blog at joelonsoftware.com. I highly recommend it. Then there are the many clients in the early days that took a chance on BerniePortal — Becky Sharpe, Dave and Lynda Huseman, Joe Cook, Steve Singleton, Randy and Kim Brooks, Rebekah Michel, Grant Barbre, Mark Henline, Cheryl Phillips, Mike Simmons, Lisa Collins, Sam Shallenberger, and so many others — without your early adoption, the product and our learning would never have gotten anywhere.

Finally, I'd like to thank BerniePortal's broker partners nationwide. The relationships we've built while serving you mean a lot to me. Furthermore, what I've learned from you has served to confirm just how local healthcare truly is in the United States and how valuable a local broker's advice can be for employers in our nation's ever-changing healthcare landscape. Thank you, as always, for your partnership.

About the Author

Driven by a passion for improving the US healthcare system, Alex Tolbert founded Bernard Health in 2006. BerniePortal, the web-based HR platform built by brokers for brokers was launched out of Bernard Health in 2008. Until 2011, Alex worked primarily as a group health insurance broker. Now, his primary duties are related to the ongoing development of BerniePortal. Originally from Indiana, Alex has his BS and BA in finance and international studies from the University of Pennsylvania (Wharton School) where he was a member of the Huntsman Program in International Studies and Business. He obtained his JD and MBA from Vanderbilt University Law School and Vanderbilt's Owen School of Management. He has passed all three levels of the CFA designation and is fluent in Spanish.